AF582206

Hurdles to Heights

A Guide to Knowing and Overcoming Workplace Obstacles and Transforming Them into Success.

NAGESH RAMAMURTHY

In halls of challenge, we rise and stand,

With trials and tests, our paths are planned.

Each hurdle met with courage and might,

Turns shadows of doubt into lessons of light.

When walls seem high and doors close tight,

Resilience becomes our guiding sight.

Through storms of struggle, we find our way,

Transforming setbacks into strength each day.

For every obstacle, a new chance to grow,

In the heart of struggle, success will show.

Dedication

They say every story has a beginning, but mine has two heartbeats.

For some, success is a lonely road, but my journey began with two extraordinary guides.

Amma and Appa, you weren't just cheerleaders on the sidelines. You were architects of possibility, showing me that every setback is a setup for a comeback. You showed me that ordinary people can achieve extraordinary things. When others saw castles in the air, you helped me build foundations under them. Your unwavering faith in my potential wasn't blind optimism – it was a profound lesson that believing in yourself isn't arrogance. It's a responsibility.

Amma, you demonstrated that resilience isn't about weathering the storm but about learning to dance in the rain.

Appa, as a true sportsman, you taught me that fear and courage are cousins and that being brave doesn't mean not being scared – it means moving forward anyway.

And to you, the reader holding this book, know that the insights I am sharing are because two people believed in someone who once stood exactly where you are now – full of doubts, dreams, and untapped potential. Whatever brought you to these pages, whatever mountain you are trying to climb, remember what someone once told me (and now I am telling you), your dreams are valid, your journey matters and your story is still being written. I am sure there will be someone who will listen to your success story one day.

This book is dedicated to the power of believing in yourself, in others, and in the magic that happens when someone loves you enough to help you spread your wings and fly.

May these pages remind you that it's never too late to begin, too early to dream, or too ambitious to try. After all, every expert was once a beginner, and every success story started with someone who refused to give up.

With a heart full of love and gratitude,

Nagesh Ramamurthy

2nd December, 2024

Preface

My motivation for writing this guide is simple – I want to provide professionals with something I wish I had – a roadmap for tackling common workplace challenges drawn from real experiences and grounded in practical advice.

Throughout my career, I was fortunate to have mentors and colleagues who shared their hard-earned wisdom with me. That guidance made all the difference in my path forward. This book is my way of paying it forward, distilling those lessons into a guide for you. My hope is that it serves as a tool to help you make more informed, confident decisions when you encounter similar challenges.

One thing you will notice as you read is that I don't dwell on abstract theories or vague suggestions. This book is intentionally practical. I believe that solutions should be straightforward and applicable, even within the complexity of corporate life.

Every chapter reflects real-world situations, covering both the day-to-day frustrations and the broader, more strategic challenges that ultimately shape a career. My goal is for this book to be your quick reference, a guide you can turn to whenever you need an objective perspective or a fresh approach to tackling an issue.

If even one chapter here provides insight or clarity when you need it most, then I will have achieved my purpose.

Thank you for allowing me to be a part of your journey. May this guide support you in transforming hurdles into milestones and in forging your own successful path forward.

Contents

Introduction

The corporate space is a minefield, and after about 35 yers in this space, I can tell you one thing for sure – **hurdles are everywhere**. But they don't have to define or limit you. Instead, they can become your stepping stones to success.

This book is about helping you see them that way – no fluff, no lengthy theories, just straight-to-the-point lessons from someone who has been through the thick of it.

If you are reading this, chances are you have encountered your share of roadblocks already, or maybe you are preparing yourself for the inevitable. The reality is whether you are a new hire, a manager, or a seasoned executive, the challenges of corporate life can be unpredictable and relentless.

I have experienced my fair share of them, from navigating office politics and dealing with uncooperative coworkers to pushing through long stretches of burnout and handling those infamous *'stretch goals.'* I won't pretend to have every answer, nor will I claim to have solved every possible challenge that exists in the workplace.

Corporate life evolves constantly, and with it, new hurdles emerge every day. However, the experiences and lessons I have chosen to share here reflect the most common hurdles that almost every professional will face, regardless of industry, seniority, or ambition. Think of them as the *'greatest hits'* of workplace hurdles – issues like managing difficult personalities, handling an overwhelming workload, keeping a cool head in politically charged environments, and more.

To be clear, this isn't an encyclopedia of every workplace problem. It's a guide to the major challenges that many of us encounter and that will, most likely, come across your path if they haven't already. These are the core challenges that can stall careers, but they are also the ones that can help propel them forward when managed with the right strategies and perspectives.

This isn't a one-size-fits-all solution manual but rather a framework that you can adapt and apply as you see fit. My aim is to offer strategies and approaches that have worked for me – and for many others – in real-world corporate situations. By sharing these experiences, I hope to give you a head start and perhaps spare you some of the setbacks I have encountered along the way.

There is no denying it, you are busy, and your time is valuable. This book is designed to be concise and to the point because I believe that solutions don't need to be buried in pages of exposition or cluttered by unnecessary complexity. I have aimed to keep each chapter clear, actionable, and direct so that you can walk away with a clear understanding of the challenge and a toolkit to handle it. Every word, every paragraph, is intended to equip you with a specific mindset or strategy. Whether you are reading this cover to cover or skimming for a particular challenge you are facing right now, this guide is structured to make it easy to find what you need quickly, apply it practically, and move forward.

I have written each chapter to focus on a single, real-world obstacle. Whether that's dealing with a difficult coworker, managing an overwhelming workload, navigating office politics, or handling feedback that's anything but constructive. These are situations that can leave you feeling frustrated, stalled, or even questioning if this corporate journey is worth it. I know because I have been there. Through trial and error and countless conversations with mentors, colleagues, and friends, I have found that the simplest, most direct solutions often work best. My hope is that you will find these insights not only relatable but genuinely helpful as you make your own way forward.

You may find some of my advice blunt or overly straightforward. But over the years, I have come to believe that most challenges, when stripped down to their core, can be addressed with straightforward solutions. For example, the importance of clear communication, setting boundaries, or knowing when to say *'no'* may seem almost too simple. Yet, these principles are often the hardest to practice and the first to fall by the wayside in a fast-paced, high-pressure environment. So, I am not here to give you overly complex formulas for success. I am here to remind you of the basics, to reinforce them, and to encourage you to apply them consistently. In my experience, it's these fundamentals that build resilience and lead to lasting, meaningful success.

You have heard these enough times, there are no shortcuts to climbing the corporate ladder, and anyone who promises otherwise is selling you something that won't last. True success – whether you define it as a title, a paycheck, or a sense of fulfillment – comes from consistently overcoming challenges, adapting to change, and learning to see setbacks as setups for future opportunities. This guide won't take away all the stress, the long hours, or the occasional frustrations of corporate life. But it can help you navigate them with confidence and purpose.

Corporate success isn't about eliminating hurdles. It's about knowing how to manage, maneuver, and sometimes even embrace them. This book is my contribution to helping you do exactly that. These are not abstract theories but practical insights I have gathered from real situations. Some of them were hard-earned, and others came from observing what works (and doesn't work) in the people around me. My aim is for you to feel equipped, maybe even inspired, to face your challenges head-on, not just to survive but to thrive.

So, as you turn the pages, know that this book isn't about reinventing the wheel. It's about making it roll more smoothly. It's a guide rooted in reality, meant to help you sidestep the pitfalls that have tripped up countless professionals before you.

You may not have all the answers by the end, but if you walk away with even one or two insights that make your path clearer, then this book will have done its job.

Welcome to your guide for transforming corporate hurdles into opportunities for growth and success.

1.

Rise Above Condescension

A glance, a tone, a word too sharp,
That cuts beneath and leaves a mark.
A heavy hand, a subtle slight,
That dims the spark, that steals the light.
But respect can heal, and pride must fall,
For we rise higher when we lift all.

'Great leaders don't talk down to others, they lift them higher.'

Let's dive into a topic that's often brushed aside but can significantly impact workplace dynamics: Condescension. You might not think much of it at first glance, but this subtle form of disrespect can create serious hurdles in professional settings. It can leave you feeling belittled or frustrated, especially when you are pouring your heart into your work and ideas. So, how do we rise above this challenge? How do we create a space where everyone feels valued and respected?

Understanding Condescension

To start, let's clarify what we mean by Condescension. It's that feeling when someone talks down to you or explains something as if you are incapable of understanding, even if you are perfectly knowledgeable about the topic at hand. Imagine you are in a meeting, passionately presenting your ideas, and someone interrupts you, breaking it down into the simplest terms. Suddenly, your enthusiasm deflates, and you feel like a child being reprimanded. It's frustrating and disheartening.

From my observations, Condescension can manifest in various ways – a patronizing tone, unnecessary explanations, or dismissive gestures. Sometimes, it's so subtle that it flies under the radar, making it all the more insidious. Often, this behavior stems from insecurity or a desire to assert power. It's a tricky hurdle that can undermine teamwork, lower morale, and stifle creativity.

The Impact of Condescension

Take a moment to understand the consequences of condescending behavior in the workplace. When Condescension goes unchecked, it can breed resentment and disengagement. Team members may become hesitant to share their ideas, fearing they will be dismissed or belittled. Innovation takes a backseat when people feel undervalued, and the overall workplace atmosphere becomes toxic.

Think about it, if you constantly feel like your contributions aren't respected, how motivated are you to give your best? The truth is, a lack of respect can lead to high turnover rates and a lack of productivity. When employees don't feel valued, there are less likely to put in extra effort or go above and beyond.

My Example

Let me take you back to a pivotal moment in my career that opened my eyes to the damaging effects of condescension.

It was a rainy Tuesday morning, and I had spent the previous week meticulously preparing for a presentation that I believed could elevate our project. The room was filled with excitement and anxiety as my colleagues and clients filed in, their faces blending anticipation and skepticism.

My heart raced with nerves and adrenaline as I stood at the front of the room. I had poured countless hours into this project, researching, and refining my ideas. I was ready to share my vision, which I believed would bring fresh energy to our team. I opened my laptop, clicked through my slides, and began to enthusiastically explain my concept, weaving in my passion for our work.

But then it happened. Just as I got to the heart of my presentation, Praveen, a well-respected senior colleague, interrupted me. *'Wait a minute, let's break this down,'* he said, his voice dripping with condescension. *I think we must understand the basics before diving deeper.'* The room went silent, and I felt the weight of his words settle like a heavy fog. It was as if he had taken my vibrant ideas and reduced them to mere child's play.

I watched him explain my points in overly simplistic terms, using phrases I had just articulated. My enthusiasm was deflated, replaced by a mix of embarrassment and frustration. I could see my colleagues' exchanging glances, some nodding while others looking uncomfortable. It was as if Praveen had drawn a line in the sand, asserting his authority while undermining mine.

As the meeting progressed, I could feel my confidence eroding. Each time I tried to interject or clarify my points, Praveen seemed to anticipate my words and cut me off, explaining them as if I were a novice. I felt like a puppet on a string, and the strings were in his hands. My heart raced not just from anxiety but from a growing determination.

When the meeting finally ended, I felt both defeated and ignited with resolve. I knew I had to confront Praveen, but how?

The thought of facing him made my stomach churn, but I was tired of feeling diminished and unheard. Gathering my courage, I approached him after the meeting. My voice trembled, but I pushed through. *'Hey, Praveen, can we talk for a minute? I value your expertise, but during the presentation, I felt my ideas were being dismissed.'*

To my surprise, he paused, his expression shifting from defensive to contemplative. *'I didn't mean to come off that way,' he admitted, a hint of humility in his voice. 'I just thought I was helping clarify things.'* I could see he didn't realize how his behavior affected me. *'I appreciate your intention, but it would really help if you let me finish my thoughts next time. I put a lot of work into this project, and I want my voice to be heard.'*

After our conversation, something shifted. Praveen nodded, his demeanor softening. *'You are right. I will be more mindful of how I communicate.'* At that moment, I felt a weight lift off my shoulders. I wasn't just standing up for myself but fostering a more respectful dialogue.

From that day forward, our dynamic changed. Praveen became more aware of his communication style, and I grew more confident in sharing my ideas. This experience taught me the importance of addressing condescension head-on. I reclaimed my voice by taking the initiative to have that difficult conversation. I paved the way for a healthier communication style within our team.

It was a powerful reminder that standing up against condescension isn't just about defending oneself but creating an environment where everyone's ideas can flourish. That rainy Tuesday taught me more than I could have imagined – it showed me that rising above condescension is a personal victory and a collective triumph.

Confronting Condescension: My Call to Action

So, what can we do about it? Whether you are on the receiving end of Condescension or finding yourself slipping into that behavior, I want to share some strategies that have worked for me in tackling this challenge head-on:

1. **Stay Calm and Composed**

   If you face Condescension, take a moment to breathe. It's easy to react defensively, but responding in anger can escalate the situation. Instead, listen actively to what is being said, and try to maintain your composure. You might say something like, *'I appreciate your perspective, but I would love to share my thoughts too.'* This approach allows you to assert yourself without starting a confrontation.

2. **Ask Clarifying Questions**

   If someone is explaining something you already understand, don't hesitate to ask questions. This can shift the focus back to your knowledge and contributions. For example, you could say, *'That's an interesting point, but I have a different viewpoint I would like to discuss.'* This technique helps reclaim the conversation and demonstrates your expertise.

3. **Set Boundaries**

   If condescending behavior persists, it's essential to establish clear boundaries. You might say, *'I value constructive feedback, but I would appreciate it if we could keep the conversation respectful.'* Setting boundaries can help create an atmosphere of mutual respect.

4. **Encourage Open Dialogue**

As a leader, fostering an environment where everyone feels comfortable sharing their thoughts is crucial. Encourage your team to voice their opinions and ideas, and make it clear that all contributions are valuable. When people feel heard, they are less likely to engage in condescending behavior.

5. **Model Respectful Communication**

Whether you are a leader or a team member, your communication style sets the tone for the workplace. Be mindful of your words and tone. Instead of talking down to others, offer constructive feedback that uplifts and encourages. Remember, true leadership is about lifting others up, not putting them down.

Building a Culture of Respect

Creating a culture of respect in the workplace requires ongoing effort. It's about more than just addressing Condescension, it's about fostering an environment where every individual feels valued and heard.

Here are a few ways I believe we can promote a culture of respect:

1. **Recognize and Celebrate Contributions**

Take the time to acknowledge the hard work and achievements of your colleagues. Celebrating successes, no matter how small, can go a long way in building a positive atmosphere. Simple gestures like shout-outs in team meetings or written notes of appreciation can reinforce a culture of respect.

2. **Foster Collaboration**

Encourage teamwork and collaboration among team members. When people work together, they develop a sense of camaraderie that can counteract condescending behavior. Create opportunities for brainstorming sessions and collaborative projects to promote a spirit of unity.

3. **Provide Training and Development**

Consider offering training on effective communication and emotional intelligence. Workshops that focus on respectful dialogue and active listening can equip team members with the tools they need to communicate effectively.

4. **Lead by Example**

If you are in a leadership position, your behavior sets the standard. Show humility and openness to feedback. When team members see you valuing their contributions and treating everyone with respect, they will be more likely to follow suit.

5. **Encourage Feedback**

Create an environment where feedback is welcomed, not feared. When team members feel comfortable giving and receiving constructive criticism, it helps build trust and respect within the group.

The Power of Empathy

At the heart of overcoming Condescension is empathy. Understanding that everyone has their own experiences and perspectives is crucial. When we approach our colleagues with empathy, we foster a sense of connection and understanding. This, in turn, creates an environment where Condescension is less likely to occur.

I encourage you to take the time to listen actively to your colleagues' viewpoints. Acknowledge their feelings and experiences, even if you don't necessarily agree. By validating their emotions, you demonstrate respect and understanding, making it less likely that they will engage in condescending behavior.

Empowering Each Other

Ultimately, overcoming Condescension is about empowerment. We have the power to lift each other up and create an inclusive workplace. By confronting condescending behavior – whether in ourselves or in others

– we can transform our work environments into spaces where everyone feels valued.

I want you to think about it, when we support each other, we are not just combating negativity. We are fostering a culture of collaboration and innovation. Everyone has something valuable to contribute, and by recognizing that, we can break down the barriers that hinder progress.

Long-Term Benefits of Overcoming Condescension

Let's consider the long-term benefits of overcoming Condescension together. When we create an environment of respect and inclusion, we unlock the full potential of our teams. Here is what we stand to gain:

1. Increased Employee Satisfaction and Retention

When employees feel valued and respected, they are more likely to be satisfied with their jobs. This satisfaction leads to higher retention rates, saving organizations the costs associated with turnover.

2. Enhanced Collaboration and Innovation

A culture that encourages open communication and respect fosters collaboration. Team members are more likely to share their ideas, leading to innovative solutions and a more creative workplace.

3. **Improved Overall Performance**

When employees feel respected and empowered, they are more likely to put forth their best effort. This heightened engagement translates to improved productivity and performance, benefiting the organization.

My Personal Reflection

As we navigate through these ideas, I encourage you to take a moment to reflect on your experiences with Condescension. Have you ever felt belittled at work? How did it make you feel? Have you ever unintentionally condescended to someone? What did you learn from that experience?

Reflection is a powerful tool for growth. By examining our behaviors and reactions, we can identify patterns that may contribute to a culture of Condescension. Recognizing our biases and tendencies allows us to consciously change and promote a more respectful workplace.

Rising Together

As we wrap up I want to remind you of your worth. You are deserving of respect, and your ideas matter. It's essential to advocate for yourself and never let anyone dim your light.

If you have ever felt the sting of Condescension, remember that you have the right to stand tall. Your ideas matter, and you deserve to be treated with respect. And if you find yourself in a position of power, take a moment to reflect. Are you fostering an environment that uplifts others? By being mindful of our words and actions, we can create a workplace where everyone thrives.

In the end, rising above Condescension isn't just about overcoming a hurdle but building heights we can all reach together. So, let's lift each other up, embrace collaboration, and tackle this challenge head-on. Together, we can transform our workplaces into vibrant, respectful spaces that empower everyone to succeed. After all, when we rise together, we create a stronger team and a brighter future for all.

By actively working to overcome Condescension, we are enhancing our experiences and paving the way for a more inclusive and empowering workplace for future generations. Let's take that step together and rise to the occasion!

'The moment we choose to be respectful, we create a space where everyone can thrive.'

2.

Respect: A Workplace Necessity

In silence, it creeps, unseen but real,
Workplace disrespect, a wound we feel.
Confidence crumbles, and self-worth fades,
In toxic shadows, potential degrades.
Yet respect can heal, with voices clear,
A culture of kindness drives out the fear.

'Every act of kindness is a piece of love we leave behind.' – Paul Williams

This topic has probably hit home for many of us at one point or another: **workplace disrespect.**

It is one of those sneaky hurdles that can hinder our productivity and mental well-being, and let me shine some light on it.

What Does Workplace Disrespect Look Like?

So, what do I mean when I say *'workplace disrespect'?*

This could manifest in various ways. Everything from being talked down to being ignored in meetings to more overt forms like bullying or harassment. Those little comments seem harmless initially, but they cut deeper than you might realize.

That snarky remark about your presentation or the coworker who constantly interrupts you. Brushing off these behaviors as *'just how things are'* or *'they didn't mean it that way can be easy.'* But trust me, these moments accumulate and can leave lasting scars.

The Effects of Disrespect

The impact of workplace disrespect isn't just emotional. It is mental, too. It can lead to increased stress, anxiety, and even depression. You might find yourself second-guessing your abilities or feeling unworthy of your position. It is not uncommon for this kind of treatment to cause a drop in self-esteem. When you constantly think belittled or overlooked, it's hard to muster the confidence to take on new challenges or speak up in meetings.

Imagine working on a big project you have poured your heart and soul into. You present your ideas to the team, feeling excited and nervous. Then, out of nowhere, a colleague laughs at your proposal, dismissing it with a condescending remark. That moment can feel like a punch in the gut. Instead of feeling proud of your hard work, you leave the meeting questioning your competence. This affects your mood for the rest of the day and can spill over into your personal life, affecting your relationships and overall happiness.

My Experience

Once, a disrespect manifested and had an impact on my mental health.

Picture this, I was bright-eyed and eager, fresh into a position at a company that I believed would be the launching pad for my dreams. The office buzzed with energy, filled with talented individuals. I felt like I was stepping into a world of opportunity.

After weeks of brainstorming and late nights crafting my proposal for a new project, I was ready to present my ideas to the team. My heart raced with nerves and excitement as I rehearsed my pitch in my mind. I believed in my vision and was eager to share it with my colleagues, hoping it would inspire them as much as it had inspired me.

As the meeting began, I felt a sense of camaraderie in the room, like we were all in this together. I laid out my proposal, detailing every aspect with enthusiasm. The room was quiet, and I could see my colleagues leaning in, some nodding along. My manager even smiled, encouraging me with a brief glance of support. I thought I was on the verge of something great.

But then, in a split second, everything shifted. As I wrapped up my presentation, the atmosphere changed dramatically. A colleague I admired for their expertise scoffed and said, *'That's not how we do things around here. Why would we even consider this?'* His words hung in the air like a thick fog, suffocating the excitement that had filled the room moments before.

The laughter that followed felt like daggers piercing through my confidence. My heart sank, and I felt heat rising to my cheeks. The supportive nods faded, replaced by a deafening silence that echoed my self-doubt. The enthusiasm I had poured into my work crumbled, and at that moment, I questioned everything. Did my idea really have no merit? Was I not cut out for this role?

As the meeting continued, I struggled to focus. Each subsequent presentation felt like a minefield, and every voice that cut across mine reminded me of that humiliating moment. My once-thriving passion began to wither, I started second-guessing my ideas and holding back in meetings. I found myself rehearsing my words over and over, afraid to say the wrong thing.

Over the following weeks, the atmosphere shifted for me. Instead of feeling like a valued team member, I felt like an outsider in a room full of talented individuals. I became increasingly withdrawn, dreading those team meetings that once inspired me. Anxiety gripped me. Each day felt heavier than the last. I could hardly sleep, often staring at the ceiling in the dark, haunted by that moment and the fear of facing my colleagues again.

The breaking point came one evening when I received a text from a friend asking me to join a social event. As I sat there staring at my phone, tears streamed down my face. I realized I had stopped enjoying the things that had once excited me about work and life. The fear of ridicule had turned me into a shell of my former self.

But a flicker of resolve ignited within me during one of those sleepless nights. I decided I could no longer let this moment define my worth. The following week, I sought a meeting with my manager. I laid bare my struggles, detailing the impact of that moment on my mental health. To my surprise, my manager listened intently, empathy shining in their eyes. They acknowledged that the culture of respect needed improvement and vowed to address it within the team.

That conversation was a turning point. With my manager's support, I began to reclaim my voice. I started sharing my ideas more boldly despite the lingering whispers of doubt. Slowly, the pieces started to fall back into place. I realized that while I could not control how others behaved, I could control my response.

This experience was a harsh but invaluable lesson. I learned that workplace disrespect doesn't just impact productivity. It has the potential to unravel a person's mental health, creativity, and self-worth. But it also taught me the power of vulnerability and the importance of advocating for a respectful workplace.

And now, as I share this story with you, I hope it resonates. Disrespect can cut deep, but it doesn't have to define your journey. By fostering a culture of respect, we can uplift ourselves and each other, creating a work environment where everyone can thrive.

The Cost of Disrespect

This experience opened my eyes to the genuine mental toll that workplace disrespect can take. I realized that treating people as if they don't matter creates a toxic environment that stifles creativity, lowers morale, and ultimately hampers productivity.

Research shows that employees who feel respected are more engaged and perform better. Conversely, those who experience disrespect can become disengaged, leading to higher turnover rates and a culture of negativity. It's a vicious cycle that can be hard to break, especially if management isn't paying attention to the signs.

Building a Respectful Workplace

So, what can we do about this? First and foremost, it's essential to foster an environment of respect. Encourage open communication and active listening among team members. If you notice disrespectful behavior, don't shy away from addressing it. Often, people may not realize the impact of their words or actions. It's all about creating a culture where everyone feels valued and heard.

If you are on the receiving end of disrespect, it's crucial to recognize the effects it's having on your mental health. Don't be afraid to reach out for support, whether talking to a mentor, friend, or professional.

Remember, you deserve to work in a respected and valued environment.

The Long-Term Benefits of a Respectful Workplace

Investing in respectful workplace culture is not just about avoiding the negative impacts of disrespect. It offers a wealth of long-term benefits for employees and the organization. Here are some key advantages –

1. **Increased Employee Engagement**

When employees feel respected and engaged and are passionate about their roles, translating into higher productivity and innovation.

2. **Improved Mental Health and Well-Being**

A respectful workplace fosters an environment where employees feel safe and valued. This significantly reduces stress and anxiety levels, leading to better mental health outcomes and lower burnout.

3. **Lower Turnover Rates**

Respectful workplaces increase job satisfaction, reducing employee turnover. When employees feel valued, they are more likely to stay long-term, saving organizations the costs associated with recruiting and training new hires.

4. Enhanced Collaboration and Teamwork

Respect fosters open communication and collaboration among team members. When employees feel comfortable expressing their ideas, it encourages teamwork, leading to more innovative solutions and effective problem-solving.

5. Stronger Organizational Culture

A culture of respect promotes positive values and behaviors that can define the organization's identity. This strong culture attracts talent and enhances the company's reputation in the industry.

6. Higher Customer Satisfaction

Employees who feel respected and happy employees often lead to happy customers, creating a positive feedback loop that drives loyalty and satisfaction.

7. Increased Productivity

Respectful environments are linked to higher productivity levels. Employees who feel valued are more focused and dedicated to their work, resulting in better quality outputs.

8. Diverse Perspectives and Innovation

In a respectful workplace, employees are likelier to share diverse perspectives without fear of judgment. This inclusion encourages creative thinking and innovation, leading to unique solutions.

9. Better Conflict Resolution

Conflicts can be addressed well when respect is ingrained in workplace culture. Employees are more likely to approach disagreements with a solution-oriented mindset, fostering a harmonious work environment.

10. Positive Employer Brand

Companies known for their respectful culture attract top talent. A positive reputation as an employer can be a significant competitive advantage in attracting and retaining skilled employees.

Final Thoughts

In wrapping up this chapter, I want to emphasize that workplace disrespect is a hurdle we can overcome together. By being aware of our words and actions and advocating for ourselves and our colleagues, we can create a healthier work environment for everyone. It's about building each other up, not tearing each other down.

If you have ever experienced disrespect in the workplace, remember you are not alone, and it's okay to feel the way you do. Your mental health matters and we all take a stand against disrespect in our work lives. Together, we can foster a culture of respect that benefits everyone involved.

'Your work is a reflection of how you treat yourself and others. Choose respect.'

3.

The Growth Barriers

When fear of failure clouds the way,
And routine keeps us stuck each day,
It's purpose found and goals in sight,
That spark the flame, rekindling light.
With courage born from deep within,
We rise, evolve, and start again.

'Personal development is the belief that you are worth the effort, time, and energy needed to develop yourself.' – Denis Waitley

We have all been there – feeling stuck, unmotivated, or even questioning our professional direction. At one point or another, most of us have experienced hurdles in personal development at work. Whether it's fear of failure, the comfort of routine, or just plain burnout, it's easy to lose that spark that pushes us forward.

But what if I told you that the key to overcoming these hurdles is not just about discipline or external rewards? It's about understanding why you do what you do. It's about tapping into those intrinsic and extrinsic motivational factors that drive personal growth and change.

Let me dive deeper into those factors and share with you how they can help you navigate challenges in the workplace.

Understanding Motivation

Motivation is the fuel behind personal development, especially in the workplace. It's why you get up in the morning and strive to be better, more skilled, and more fulfilled in your career. Two key types of Motivation influence your behavior: **extrinsic and intrinsic**.

Extrinsic Motivation comes from external factors – rewards like a paycheck, recognition, promotions, or avoiding negative consequences (like being fired). While these motivators can be powerful, they are often short-lived. For example, you might work extra hard for a bonus, but the Motivation fades away once you have got it.

Intrinsic Motivation comes from within. It's when you pursue personal growth because it brings you satisfaction, fulfillment, or a sense of purpose. Maybe you love learning new things, solving problems, or contributing to a more significant cause. This kind of Motivation has a lasting impact because it connects deeply with who you are and what matters to you.

Both types of Motivation play essential roles, but intrinsic Motivation is often the secret sauce that leads to sustainable personal development.

Common Workplace Hurdles to Personal Development

Even when we are motivated, workplace challenges can derail our efforts. Let's look at some common hurdles that people face –

1. Fear of Failure

Many of us are held back by the fear of failing. We avoid taking on new projects or learning new skills because we fear making mistakes or looking incompetent. This fear creates a stagnant environment where personal development stalls.

But here is the truth: Failure is part of growth. It's through making mistakes that we learn the most. I have failed, gathered myself and continued my journey.

When you fall, get up and restart, you will find that your restart is 2 steps from where you fell. Your fall has still given you a bit of progress.

Manjunath, a mid-level manager, was offered a leadership role to head a new department but turned down out of fear that he wasn't 'qualified enough.' Even though he knew it would be a massive opportunity for personal and professional growth, his fear of failure outweighed his intrinsic desire to develop new skills. As a result, Manjunath remained in his comfort zone, frustrated by the lack of progress in her career.

Eventually, Manjunath realized that avoiding challenges was limiting his growth. He gradually overcame his fear by shifting his mindset and taking small, manageable risks. Now, he embraces learning through trial and error, knowing that mistakes are a stepping stone to success.

2. Lack of Clarity or Direction

Sometimes, we feel unmotivated because we are unsure where we are headed. Personal development can seem like an abstract, distant concept without a clear vision or goals. You might be putting in the effort at work, but if you don't know why you are doing it, progress can feel hollow and unrewarding.

What to do?

Setting clear, actionable goals is critical. It's not just about doing more.

It's about doing the right things that align with your aspirations and values.

3. Burnout and Overwork

Burnout is a significant hurdle to personal development. How can you focus on improving yourself if you are constantly overwhelmed, overworked, and running on empty? Personal development requires energy, creativity, and focus – things in short supply when burnt out.

Burnout often leads to a vicious cycle where the more overwhelmed you feel, the less motivated you are to act, leading to stagnation and disengagement.

Nitin worked long hours as a marketing director, juggling multiple projects and managing a large team. Though he was outwardly successful, internally, he was running on fumes.

He wanted to develop his leadership skills, take professional courses, and spend more time mentoring younger employees. But the constant grind left him too exhausted to pursue these personal development goals.

Eventually, Nitin took a step back and reassessed his workload. He negotiated with his employer to delegate more tasks, set boundaries for work hours, and carved out time in his week to focus on personal growth.

This shift allowed him to reignite his passion for his work and begin pursuing the development goals that mattered most to him.

Motivational Factors that Drive Personal Development

Now that we have identified the hurdles let's explore the motivational factors that can help you overcome them and push through to the next level of growth:

1. Purpose and Meaning

One of the strongest drivers of intrinsic Motivation is the sense of purpose. When you feel that your work aligns with your values and contributes to something meaningful, your desire for personal development flourishes.

Ask yourself:

- Why do I want to grow?
- How does my personal development contribute to my broader life goals and values?

Understanding your purpose will give you the energy to overcome challenges because you will know that your efforts lead to something bigger.

2. Autonomy

Having control over your own decisions can significantly impact your Motivation to grow. When you feel empowered to take charge of your learning and career path, you will likely seek new opportunities and embrace challenges.

If you are in a role where autonomy is limited, look for areas where you can take initiative, even in small ways. This could mean volunteering for a new project or suggesting ways to improve existing processes. The key is to create a sense of ownership over your personal growth.

3. Mastery

Humans are naturally wired to want to improve and get better at things. The desire for mastery is a powerful motivator for personal development. Whether it's learning a new skill, deepening your expertise, or becoming a leader in your field, the pursuit of mastery can push you past workplace hurdles.

To tap into this motivator, set specific, achievable goals that will help you grow incrementally. For example, instead of aiming to *'be a better leader,'* set a goal to *'attend a leadership workshop'* or *'mentor a junior colleague.'* These smaller, tangible steps help build the foundation for long-term growth.

4. Supportive Environment

The environment you work in plays a significant role in your ability to develop. A workplace that encourages growth, values feedback, and supports learning will naturally foster personal development. However, in environments where personal development isn't a priority, it can be challenging to stay motivated.

If you are in a workplace that doesn't prioritize growth, seek out mentors or colleagues who do. Building your support network can sometimes provide the encouragement and accountability you need.

In her early career, Vidya worked with me where professional development wasn't emphasized. It was a 'get the job done and go home' type of culture, which left her feeling stifled and unfulfilled. However, instead of resigning to her circumstances, she contacted a mentor from a different department who shared her passion for growth.

With his guidance and support, Vidya found ways to improve her skills outside her immediate role, eventually paving the way for a promotion and a more fulfilling career path.

Taking Ownership of Your Development

Motivational factors are the driving force behind personal development, especially when workplace hurdles get in the way. To overcome these hurdles, you need to understand what truly motivates you. Is it the sense of purpose, the pursuit of mastery, or the autonomy to make your own decisions? Once you identify these factors, you can align them with your daily actions and long-term goals.

It's important to remember that personal development is not a one-time event but a continuous journey. There will always be setbacks, challenges, and periods of stagnation. But by staying connected to your purpose and surrounding yourself with a supportive environment, you can push through even the most challenging workplace hurdles.

Remember, personal development is **an investment** in you – and the rewards are far greater than any paycheck or promotion.

'Your journey of personal growth begins the moment you decide that staying the same is no longer an option.'

4.

Overcoming Reflective Barriers

In the rush of daily tasks,
We often forget to pause and ask,
Am I growing, am I stuck?
What lessons hide beneath the muck?
Through reflection's honest light,
We find the strength to rise and fight

'Growth begins when we start to question our own assumptions, and self-reflection is the path that leads us to our greatest potential.'

Friends, as we wrap up our discussion on growth, it's clear that taking care of our growth is crucial for thriving in both our personal and professional lives.

One essential component of nurturing that growth is self-reflection. It's not just a trendy concept. It's a powerful tool that can help us navigate the complexities of the workplace while fostering our personal development.

I touch this topic more often.

Why Self-Reflection Matters

Self-reflection is the practice of stepping back from our daily grind to evaluate our thoughts, feelings, and actions. It's like taking a moment to pause in a fast-paced race to check your map and adjust your direction if necessary. In the hustle and bustle of the workplace, we often forget to check in with ourselves. However, self-reflection is what helps us understand our motivations, recognize our strengths and weaknesses, and ultimately guide our growth.

The Connection to Growth

Now, let's talk about growth. Self-reflection isn't just a moment of contemplation. It's an active process that fuels our development. When we take the time to reflect, we create opportunities to learn from our experiences – both good and bad. This understanding allows us to set actionable goals, adapt our behaviors, and foster resilience in the face of challenges.

Why Self-Reflection and Growth is a Workplace Challenge

Despite its importance, self-reflection and growth can be significant challenges in the workplace. Here are a few reasons why:

1. Fast-Paced Environment

In today's work culture, where deadlines loom and tasks pile up, it's easy to get caught in a cycle of constant activity. Many of us are so busy *'doing'* that we forget to pause and reflect. This can lead to burnout, decreased motivation, and a lack of clear direction.

2. Fear of Vulnerability

Self-reflection often requires us to confront uncomfortable truths about ourselves – our weaknesses, mistakes, and areas for improvement. This can be a daunting process, especially in a competitive workplace where individuals may fear that admitting shortcomings could harm their reputation or career prospects.

3. Lack of Support

Not everyone works in a supportive environment that encourages self-reflection. Suppose leaders and colleagues don't prioritize feedback or growth. In that case, it can create a culture where employees feel isolated in their struggles. Without a supportive network, the process of reflection can feel daunting and ineffective.

4. Limited Time and Resources

Many organizations don't allocate time or resources for personal development. Employees may feel pressured to prioritize immediate tasks over long-term growth, leading to a cycle of stagnation where self-reflection takes a backseat.

5. Resistance to Change

Change is often uncomfortable, and self-reflection can highlight the need for changes in habits, routines, or behaviors. This resistance can make it challenging to embrace growth opportunities, as people may cling to familiar patterns – even if they aren't serving them well.

A Personal Story

Let me share a personal story that illustrates how self-reflection can drive growth. A few years ago, I was managing a project that was, to put it mildly, spiraling out of control. Deadlines were missed, team morale was low, and I felt like I was constantly putting out fires instead of leading.

At first, I pointed fingers – at the team, the clients, and even the coffee machine that seemed to be malfunctioning at the worst possible times. I was overwhelmed, stressed, and completely at a loss for how to turn things around. But one evening, after a particularly chaotic day, I decided to take a step back and engage in some self-reflection. I grabbed my notebook and started writing.

I asked myself a few key questions:

- What went wrong?
- How did I contribute to these issues?
- What could I have done differently?

As I reflected, I realized that I had been so focused on meeting deadlines that I had neglected the importance of communication. I hadn't set clear expectations with my team, nor had I checked in regularly to see how everyone was feeling about their workload. Instead of fostering collaboration, I had created an environment where everyone felt overwhelmed and unsupported.

The Impact of Self-Reflection

This realization hit me hard. I was the captain of the ship, and I hadn't even bothered to check the sails! But this moment of self-reflection became the turning point for me. I recognized that my stress and anxiety were not just personal burdens, they were also impacting my team's morale and productivity.

After that night of reflection, I initiated a team meeting to discuss our challenges openly. I apologized for my oversight and encouraged everyone to share their thoughts on how we could improve our processes. To my surprise, the response was overwhelmingly positive. My team appreciated my vulnerability and was eager to contribute.

We established a weekly check-in, redefined our roles, and created a collaborative environment where everyone felt empowered to speak up. The result? We not only met our next deadline, but we also completed the project ahead of schedule!

Building a Culture of Self-Reflection

This experience taught me that self-reflection is not just a personal endeavor, it's something we can cultivate within our teams and organizations. When we model self-assessment and honesty, we encourage others to do the same. It creates a culture of openness where feedback is welcomed, and growth becomes a shared journey.

Practical Steps to Foster Self-Reflection and Growth

So, how can you integrate self-reflection into your daily routine?

Here are some practical steps:

1. **Set Aside Time**

Just like you schedule meetings, block off time on your calendar for self-reflection. It doesn't have to be long – 15 minutes a day can work wonders.

2. Ask the Right Questions

Use prompts to guide your reflection. Some examples include:

- What were my most significant accomplishments this week?
- What challenges did I face, and how did I respond?
- What did I learn from my experiences?
- How did my emotions affect my actions and decisions?

3. Journaling

Writing down your thoughts can clarify your feelings and make them more manageable. It also creates a record you can revisit to see how much you have grown over time.

4. Seek Feedback

Sometimes, it's hard to see ourselves clearly. Ask colleagues for constructive feedback. Be open to their insights – they can provide a different perspective that can be incredibly valuable.

5. Set Goals

After reflecting, set actionable goals. What do you want to achieve in the short and long term? Be specific and measurable.

6. Celebrate Progress

Growth takes time, so celebrate your achievements, no matter how small. Recognizing progress reinforces the importance of self-reflection and its role in personal development.

Final Thoughts

In conclusion, self-reflection and growth are not just buzzwords. They are essential skills that can transform your professional life and enhance your overall well-being.

By taking the time to evaluate your actions, thoughts, and feelings, you set yourself on a path toward improvement and fulfillment. Remember, it's okay to stumble along the way.

What matters is that you pick yourself up, learn from your experiences, and keep moving forward.

'True growth happens not when we avoid our mistakes, but when we embrace them, reflect on them, and use them as stepping stones to become better versions of ourselves.'

5.

Turbulence in Teamwork

In teams we strive, yet hurdles arise,
Missteps and silence cloud the skies.
Trust is fragile, but must be earned,
Through open hearts and lessons learned.
With every voice and hand in play,
We build together, day by day.

'Coming together is a beginning, keeping together is progress, working together is success.' – Henry Ford

Let's be honest for a second. When you think about your daily work life, what is one thing that can either make or break your day? I bet that most of you would say, ***'My team.'*** Whether you work with a small group or a large department, the people you collaborate with can significantly influence your motivation, productivity, and overall experience.

Regardless of the industry, one of the biggest hurdles many of us face is navigating team dynamics and fostering positive team behaviors.

So, why is this such a common challenge? We all bring our personalities, expectations, and experiences to the workplace, and blending those differences to create a harmonious, productive environment is easier said than done. But it's so important.

What Do We Mean by 'Positive Team Behaviors'?

Before we dive deeper, let's clarify what we mean by positive team behaviors. These are the kinds of actions and attitudes that contribute to a healthy and functional work environment. Things like:

- **Open Communication:** People feel comfortable sharing their ideas, concerns, and feedback.

- **Mutual respect:** Every team member values each other's contributions, regardless of their role.
- **Support and collaboration:** There is a genuine sense of *'we are in this together'* rather than competing.
- **Accountability:** Everyone takes responsibility for their actions, and there is no finger-pointing when things go wrong.
- **Constructive conflict resolution:** Disagreements happen, but they are handled professionally and productively.

Why Are These Behaviors So Hard to Build?

Let's face it. Teams are made up of human beings – complex, sometimes unpredictable, and always unique. People have their own stressors, communication styles, and ways of working. In my experience, one of the biggest obstacles is getting everyone on the same page, especially regarding Communication and expectations.

At one point in my career, I worked on a technically solid project team. We had experts in different fields. On paper, we should have been unstoppable. But something wasn't clicking. Meetings were unproductive, people weren't speaking up, and it felt like we were working in silos rather than as a cohesive unit. At first, I couldn't figure out what was wrong, but over time, it became clear our Communication was off. No one felt comfortable enough to share when they were stuck, and there was a lot of passive-aggressive tension. We were working around each other rather than with each other.

The turning point came when we decided to have an open conversation about our team dynamics. It wasn't easy – people had to own up to some uncomfortable truths – but we made real progress once we addressed the elephant in the room. We established more explicit expectations for Communication and accountability, which turned things around.

Common Workplace Hurdles When Building Positive Team Behaviors

1. Lack of Trust

Trust is the bedrock of any positive team dynamic. When there's no trust, everything else falls apart. Think about it: If you don't trust your teammates, will you give them candid feedback? Will you be willing to admit when you have made a mistake? Probably not.

2. Poor Communication

One person thinks they have been clear, but the other completely misunderstands. This happens more often than we think. Miscommunication can lead to frustration, missed deadlines, and even damaged relationships within the team. And the kicker?

It's usually preventable with better listening and more explicit articulation.

3. Unclear Roles and Expectations

When people don't know what's expected of them, it creates confusion and resentment.

I have seen teams where tasks fall through the cracks simply because no one knew who was responsible. Conversely, when expectations are clear, teams can function like well-oiled machines.

4. Resistance to feedback

Feedback is crucial for improvement, but many people feel attacked when they receive it.

Positive team behaviours include giving feedback constructively and being willing to accept it without becoming defensive.

5. Lack of Diversity in Thought and Approach

When everyone in a team thinks alike, it can lead to groupthink, where new ideas are stifled. On the other hand, when team members bring different perspectives, it can lead to richer discussions and better solutions.

But diversity in thought requires an environment where people feel comfortable expressing dissenting opinions – and that's not always easy to create.

Strategies for Building Positive Team Behaviors

1. Create a Culture of Openness and Transparency

Encourage open dialogue in your team. It's essential that people feel safe expressing their thoughts and concerns without fear of backlash. This can be done through regular check-ins, feedback sessions, or even informal conversations. In my experience, scheduling a *'team pulse'* meeting – where the sole purpose was to discuss how we felt about the team's dynamics – worked wonders. This helped us proactively address minor issues before they ballooned into more significant problems.

2. Encourage Vulnerability

This might sound counterintuitive, especially in a professional setting. Still, when leaders and team members show Vulnerability, it humanizes them and builds trust. Sharing when you have made a mistake or admitting that you don't have all the answers makes others more willing to do the same. Vulnerability doesn't mean oversharing, it means creating a space where authenticity is valued over perfection.

3. Set Clear Roles and Expectations

When roles and responsibilities are clearly defined, it reduces ambiguity. Make sure each team member knows exactly what is expected of them. This also means establishing shared goals – when everyone understands the bigger picture, it's easier to see how their individual contributions fit in. During a project I led, we created a shared document that outlined every task, who was responsible, and deadlines. It was a simple move, but it transformed our efficiency and accountability.

4. Practice Active Listening

Active listening goes beyond just hearing words – understanding their intent. People are often more concerned with what they will say next than hearing what the other person is saying. By practicing active listening, you can ensure everyone feels heard, which leads to more vital collaboration.

5. Celebrate Small Wins and Progress

Positive reinforcement goes a long way in shaping team behaviors. Celebrate small victories and progress, not just the final result. This helps in building a sense of achievement and motivation to keep improving.

6. Invest in Team Building Activities

Sometimes, breaking away from the work environment can be the best thing for a team. Team building exercises – whether there are formal workshops or casual outings – can help build trust and improve Communication. During one of our most challenging projects, our team participated in a retreat that included activities designed to foster collaboration and problem-solving. It gave us a fresh perspective on each other's strengths and communication styles.

A Turning Point in My Own Team

Let me take you back to when I led a cross-functional team on a project that should have been a career highlight. We had talented, experienced people from different departments – marketing, operations, product development, and finance. Each one of us had specific expertise and was excited to contribute. But, as the weeks passed, that excitement started fading, and something felt off.

At first, the issues were subtle – missed deadlines, miscommunication over emails, and the occasional passive-aggressive remark in meetings. But nothing major, right? We all just chalked it up to typical workplace stress. Everyone was busy, deadlines were tight, and pressures were high. But soon enough, things began to spiral.

Team members started retreating into their own corners. Communication was happening less and less. When it did happen, it was tense, formal, and transactional. Meetings felt more like necessary evils than spaces for collaboration. We were working in isolation, even though we were supposed to be a team. I could feel it – things were on the verge of falling apart.

I will never forget this one meeting. It was meant to be a simple status update. We all walked into the conference room with that familiar tension hanging in the air. The meeting was quiet, too quiet. The marketing lead started running through the progress on their part of the project.

Still, the operations lead immediately cut in with a frustrated tone: *'That's not what we agreed on last week. You are way off track.'* The room went cold. The marketing leads stiffened, visibly annoyed, and shot back, *'If you would checked the email I sent, you would know this is exactly where we should be.'*

I have been in tough meetings before, but this one had a different vibe. People weren't just disagreeing, it felt like our trust had eroded entirely. And suddenly, it hit me – we were headed straight for disaster.

The worst part? This wasn't a one-off exchange. It was a symptom of a more significant problem, a slow burn that had been simmering for weeks. Everyone was frustrated, confused, and burned out, but no one wanted to admit it. We were all pointing fingers, silently blaming each other for the project not moving forward, when, in reality, it was *'all of us.'*

The Breaking Point

That meeting was a pivotal moment for me as a leader. We were on the verge of a full-on blow-up, and I knew that if we didn't do something now, the project – and potentially the relationships we had built would collapse. After that meeting, I decided to call for a team-wide intervention, though I didn't use the word *'intervention'* at the time. That would have just freaked people out.

Instead, I framed it as an informal *'team alignment'* meeting. But I was nervous. Would people show up? Would they actually talk openly? Or would it be just another round of finger-pointing and passive-aggressive remarks? I couldn't predict how it would go, but I knew we had to try something different.

I sent out the invite for the meeting with a purposely vague agenda. It said, *'Let's talk about how we are working as a team, not just the project.'* No one said anything about it, but I could tell from people's eyes that they were apprehensive. No one likes these types of conversations. And honestly, I wasn't sure it was going to work either. I spent the next few days feeling the weight of anticipation, hoping this meeting wouldn't backfire and make things worse.

The Day of the Meeting

Everyone sat around the table, and the tension was palpable. I decided to start by acknowledging the elephant in the room. *'Guys,'* I began, *'I think we can all feel things aren't going as smoothly as we would like. This project has been tough, but we haven't really talked about how we are working together.'*

There was silence. I could feel the skepticism, and my own anxiety started rising. My mind was racing with thoughts like, *'What if they don't open up? What if I lose control of this conversation?'* But I knew I had to endure the discomfort, so I continued.

'I want this meeting to be a place where we can be honest, sincere, about what's working and what isn't. No blame, no judgment. Just how we are feeling.'

Another long pause. I thought, This is it. They are not going to talk. But then, to my surprise, someone broke the silence. The operations lead was the same person who had clashed with marketing in the previous meeting. He said, *'I will start. Honestly, I have been frustrated. I feel like I am in the dark half the time. I am not getting the information I need when I need it, and I don't know how to fix it.'*

And the floodgates opened.

The marketing lead, the same one who had snapped back at him, took a deep breath, and said, *'I didn't realize you were feeling that way. I have been working late nights to keep up, and when I don't hear back from you or anyone else, I feel like I am carrying this whole thing alone.'*

Suddenly, what had felt like personal attacks started to sound more like shared frustrations. As more people began to speak, I realized that no one was against each other. Everyone was just overwhelmed and felt disconnected. We were working in silos, not because we wanted to, but because we didn't know how to communicate better or collaborate more effectively.

The Turning Point

I could feel the energy in the room shifting as we continued the conversation. What started as tense confessions transformed into a constructive dialogue. People weren't just venting but actively trying to understand each other's pain points. It was a breakthrough moment we hadn't planned for but desperately needed.

The breakthrough didn't happen because we solved all our problems in that meeting. No, that wasn't the case. But what we accomplished was far more critical. Everyone left that room knowing that things had to be different, and more importantly, we now had a shared sense of ownership over how they needed to change.

After that meeting, we agreed on a few concrete steps. First, we committed to having regular *'team pulse'* check-ins, not to talk about the project itself, but to talk about how we were working as a team. Second, we made a pact to communicate more openly, even if that meant uncomfortable conversations. And third, we decided to set more explicit expectations around roles and responsibilities. Hence, no one felt like they were working alone in the dark.

The Impact

Over the next few weeks, the difference was night and day. Meetings were still challenging, deadlines were still tight, but the passive-aggressiveness vanished. People started asking for help when needed rather than waiting until they were completely overwhelmed. The project began moving forward much faster because we weren't spending all our energy managing miscommunication or unspoken frustrations. Most importantly, trust began to rebuild. We didn't have to love every moment of the project. Still, we respected each other's contributions and felt more like a unified team.

Today, when I look back, that meeting was the turning point for the project, and I see how I viewed leadership and team dynamics. I learned that no amount of talent or expertise can make up for broken Communication and mistrust. More importantly, I realized that sometimes, the most difficult conversations are the ones that lead to the most significant breakthroughs.

Final Thoughts

That experience taught me something invaluable. The hardest thing to do is often necessary when leading a team, especially in challenging situations. It would have been easy to ignore the tension, to let people keep working in silos and hope the project would somehow turn out fine.

Authentic leadership and teamwork require stepping into discomfort and creating space for open, honest conversations. That's when the magic happens.

So, if you are ever in a similar position – where things are not working, and you can't figure out why – don't wait for the tension to explode. Be the one to address it.

Yes, it's uncomfortable, but the potential for real change lies in that discomfort.

'Alone we can do so little, together we can do so much.' – Helen Keller

6.

Tackling Workplace Change

When change arrives, the winds may shift,
Uncertainty stirs, hearts start to drift.
But clear words can light the way,
Turning doubt to hope each day.
With open ears and steady guide,
Together, through the storm, we will glide.

'The art of communication is the language of leadership.' – James Humes

'Change is coming.'

Those three words can send shockwaves through any workplace.

Suddenly, the familiar routines are disrupted, uncertainty looms, and anxiety sets in.

It's not the change that creates the most chaos – it's the lack of clear communication. When the message isn't right, what could have been a smooth transition turns into confusion, resistance, and a productivity nosedive. How you talk about change can make the difference between a team that feels empowered and blindsided.

So, how do you navigate this storm?

Let's break it down.

The Need for Communication During Change

Change can trigger uncertainty, anxiety, or even resistance among employees. For many people, the comfort of the familiar is what makes work manageable. Once that's threatened, it's natural for doubts and concerns to rise to the surface. When the purpose and process of change are not communicated well, employees may feel alienated or, worse, completely disengaged.

At its core, communication during change isn't just about delivering information. It's about framing that change in a way that employees can connect. It's about acknowledging their fears and frustrations while showing them why the change is necessary and how it benefits them.

My Workplace Change Story

A few years ago, my company introduced a new software system to replace our outdated database. The shift promised to be more efficient and save us tedious work hours. From the leadership's perspective, it was a no-brainer. However, from the employees' perspective, it was an entirely different story.

For many on the team, the old system had been in place for years, and they had become deeply familiar with it, even though it had many flaws. The initial reaction to the announcement was anger. Why should the company invest a fortune? It could be used for the welfare of its people, maybe a higher increment, a decent bonus, or higher perks. Along with it also came anxiety. My colleagues were worried they wouldn't be able to learn the new system or their productivity would plummet during the transition. These fears, left unaddressed, quickly turned into resistance.

This is where communication (or, in this case, lack of it) played a significant role. Leadership initially assumed that simply announcing the change and providing basic training would be enough. Leaders did not take the time to fully explain why this investment for change was happening, nor did Leaders address the team's concerns about the steep learning curve.

The result?

The outcome is confusion, frustration, and a drop in morale.

However, when leadership realized this, they adjusted their communication strategy. They started holding regular Q&A sessions, where employees could voice their concerns directly. Managers tried to sit down with team members one-on-one to explain how the new system would make their day-to-day work easier. They also brought in more resources to support the transition – such as extended training sessions and precise documentation.

With this change in communication strategy, people began to feel heard, and as a result, the resistance eased. Employees started to see the new system not as an imposition but as a tool that could help them. The transition wasn't without its bumps, but the improvement in communication created a much smoother path.

Breaking Down the Communication Strategies

Let's look at the communication strategies that can help navigate changes in the workplace more effectively, using insights from both my experience and best practices.

1. Start with a Clear Vision

One of the most critical first steps is to clearly understand why the change is happening. This is where leadership often falters. It's not enough to say, *'This is happening because we need to improve productivity.'* You need to explain the why in a way that resonates with everyone.

Ask yourself:

- How will this change make the team's work easier?
- What challenges are we currently facing that this change addresses?
- What will success look like after the change is fully implemented?

For example, if a company is implementing a new project management tool, explaining that it will streamline communication and eliminate duplicate work might help employees understand its value rather than view it as just another learning task.

2. Open Channels of Dialogue

As with my story, one of the biggest mistakes is one-way communication. Simply telling people that a change is happening isn't enough. Employees need to feel like they can ask questions, voice concerns, and even give input.

Here's how you can do that:

- Hold Q&A sessions: Create forums where employees can ask questions anonymously in a group setting
- One-on-One check-ins: Sometimes, people are more comfortable sharing their concerns

privately. Managers should make time for these one-on-one conversations.

- Surveys and feedback loops: If the change is particularly complex, surveys or feedback forms can help gauge employee sentiment and adjust strategies accordingly.

3. Acknowledge the Challenges

When communicating change, don't gloss over the difficulties. Being upfront about the challenges employees may face shows empathy and builds trust. You are not trying to sell the change like a product – you are acknowledging that while the transition may be challenging, resources and support are available.

For instance, saying, *'We know learning this new system may initially feel overwhelming. That's why we are providing extra training and support to help you through it,'* and we can reassure employees that their struggles are being considered.

4. Provide Training and Support

Even the best-planned changes will fall flat if employees don't feel adequately prepared. Clear, ongoing training is essential for successful implementation. A quick, two-hour training session probably won't be enough if the change is complex. People learn differently, so provide different types of support–detailed documentation, video tutorials, hands-on sessions, and accessible help.

From my experience, the turning point came when the company began offering extended training sessions. Employees were initially reluctant, but the additional support made them feel more confident and engaged.

5. Celebrate Wins (Even Small Ones)

Change doesn't happen overnight. As progress is made, it's important to celebrate milestones, even small ones. Recognizing when teams or individuals adapt well to the change can build momentum and motivate others to do the same.

In the case of the new software we implemented, management tried to highlight team members who were mastering the system quickly and using it to streamline their work. This positive reinforcement encouraged others to keep pushing through the learning curve.

6. Maintain Transparency Throughout the Process

Even after the change is underway, keep the communication flowing. Employees will want to know how the transition is progressing and what's coming next. Share the successes and be transparent about any challenges or delays. This level of openness fosters trust and keeps everyone engaged in the process.

Why It All Matters

Effective communication strategies during times of change can make or break a transition. When communication is clear, consistent, and compassionate, employees feel supported. They are more likely to embrace the change rather than resist it. This leads to smoother transitions, higher morale, and a more successful outcome.

Final Thoughts

Change is hard – there is no getting around that. But the way we communicate through that change can make all the difference. We can guide employees through transitions with empathy and effectiveness by offering a clear vision, engaging in open dialogue, supporting, and celebrating progress.

Remember, every workplace is different, and so is every change. But no matter the situation, communication is the key to ensuring that change isn't something to fear but can propel your team and your organization forward.

'Change is hard at first, messy in the middle, but gorgeous at the end.' – Robin Sharma

7.

Breaking Bias Barrier

In every voice, a story untold,
Inclusion breaks the silent mold.
Differences spark, like stars in the night,
But fear of change can dim their light.
Embrace each thread, weave strong and true,
A diverse workplace begins with you.

'Strength lies in differences, not in similarities.' – Stephen R. Covey

When it comes to diversity and inclusion in the workplace, the idea itself is often seen as a given – who wouldn't want a workplace where everyone feels valued, regardless of their background, race, gender, religion, or any other defining characteristic? But when you dig beneath the surface, you quickly realize that while most people agree on the importance of diversity and inclusion in theory, putting it into practice can be a real challenge.

Let's discuss why that's and how we can embrace it to create an environment where everyone feels they belong.

Why Is Diversity and Inclusion So Important?

Before we dive into the challenges, let's establish why diversity and inclusion matter in the workplace.

A diverse workforce isn't just a *'feel-good'* measure – it's good business. It brings different perspectives, fosters innovation, and challenges groupthink. Imagine you are working on a project with five other people who all think the same way, come from similar backgrounds, and share similar experiences. Chances are, your final product will be narrow in scope because you have all approached it from a similar angle.

Imagine if your team included people from different cultural backgrounds, gender identities, age groups, or life experiences. Each person would bring their unique perspective to the table, and the result would be much richer, creative, and innovative.

But inclusion? That's where the real magic happens. You can hire the most diverse group in the world. Still, diversity will fail to deliver its benefits if your workplace doesn't make them feel included, valued, and heard. Inclusion ensures that everyone feels they belong and can contribute authentically without fear of being judged, ignored, or overlooked.

The Common Hurdle: Resistance to Change

The tricky part is that embracing diversity and inclusion faces resistance, even if unintentional.

People are creatures of habit. Many of us find comfort in the familiar. Whether we realize it or not, we tend to gravitate toward people like us. It's easy to fall into routines where we surround ourselves with similar people without considering what we might miss out on.

In my own experience, I have seen how these challenges play out in real life.

At a previous job, I worked with a small team in a very homogeneous company – most of us were from the same region, had similar educational backgrounds, and shared the same social interests. Things were comfortable, sure. However, things became a bit bumpy when the company decided to diversify by hiring more employees from different backgrounds and with different skill sets.

We would have meetings where people from diverse backgrounds try to share their perspectives. Still, there was subtle resistance from some of the original team members. No one was outwardly hostile, but there were eye rolls, dismissive remarks, and an unspoken sense of *'we have always done it this way.'* Clearly, the diverse voices were not being valued the same way as others.

I remember one situation where a newly hired colleague – let's call her Sonam – proposed a new approach to solving a client issue based on her experience in a different country. The rest of the team, all from a similar background, was skeptical. They didn't outright say they didn't like the idea. Still, they kept finding reasons why it wouldn't work without genuinely listening to the unique perspective she was bringing.

This kind of resistance isn't always intentional. It's rooted in unconscious biases, habits, and fear of change. This is a very common hurdle in embracing diversity and inclusion: people are not always aware of their biases or how they might be pushing others away.

Addressing the Hurdles: The Power of Awareness

Overcoming these hurdles starts with awareness. Let me share a few insights that helped our team and can help any workplace struggling with embracing diversity:

1. **Acknowledge Biases**

We all have unconscious biases. The key is recognizing them so we can actively work against them. For example, in my team, we realized that most of us had biases around valuing experiences that looked like our own, which led to dismissing ideas from colleagues with different backgrounds.

2. Create Safe Spaces for Discussion

One of the first steps in breaking down resistance is creating spaces where people can discuss their experiences and ideas without fear of judgment. This doesn't mean forcing people into uncomfortable conversations but encouraging open dialogue. For us, this meant setting aside time in meetings to hear from people whose perspectives were typically less represented.

3. Lead by Example

Leadership plays a huge role in fostering inclusion. If leaders don't model inclusive behavior – like listening to all voices in a meeting or openly acknowledging their learning curves – the rest of the team won't prioritize inclusion. In my case, when our team lead began actively inviting more input from our diverse colleagues, it set a new standard for the rest of us.

4. Embrace the Learning Curve

No one is immediately perfect at diversity and inclusion. There will be mistakes, awkward conversations, and moments where you might feel uncomfortable. But that's part of the process. We had to learn to be okay with making mistakes as long as we moved toward a more inclusive environment.

The Impact of Inclusion: A Real-Life Shift

Over time, our team began to shift. It wasn't easy or instant. It took real effort, but eventually, people realized the value of listening to different perspectives. Initially met with skepticism, Sonam's ideas started to resonate once we gave them a fair shot. Her approach was exactly what we needed to solve a recurring problem with a particular client.

This was a turning point. We started actively seeking input from people we had unintentionally overlooked before. And guess what? It led to better results. We were more innovative and adaptable, and our clients noticed the difference. People who once felt sidelined now felt empowered to contribute, and that empowerment rippled through the team.

Practical Tips for Embracing Diversity and Inclusion

If you want to start embracing diversity and inclusion in your workplace, here are a few practical steps you can take:

1. **Evaluate Your Hiring Practices**

Are you actively seeking diverse candidates, or are you stuck in a loop of hiring people who look and think like you? Widen your net when looking for talent and challenge yourself to consider candidates from non-traditional backgrounds.

2. **Develop Inclusive Policies**

Make sure your workplace policies reflect your commitment to inclusion – offering flexibility for parents, supporting mental health, or making accommodations for people with disabilities. Policies are a tangible way to show your team that inclusion isn't just talk.

3. **Provide Ongoing Training**

Regular diversity and inclusion training can help your team become more aware of biases, learn about different cultures, and develop communication skills effectively in a diverse environment. It's not just a one-off event, it's a continuous learning process.

4. **Celebrate Differences**

Make a habit of celebrating different cultures, perspectives, and experiences. Whether hosting cultural events, recognizing essential holidays, or simply encouraging employees to share parts of their identity with the team, celebrating differences helps normalize diversity and fosters a sense of belonging.

The Long-Term Benefit

Embracing diversity and inclusion isn't just a trendy buzzword for businesses. It's essential to create a workplace where people thrive, ideas flourish, and innovation becomes the norm. But it's not without its challenges. Resistance to change, unconscious biases, and the comfort of sticking with *'what we know'* are all hurdles you will likely face.

But the reward?

A team where everyone feels valued, heard, and empowered to bring their best selves to work. The journey to creating a genuinely inclusive environment may be arduous. Still, the long-term benefits – better collaboration, more creativity, and more tremendous success – are absolutely worth it.

After all, it's not just about adding diversity into the mix. It is about ensuring that everyone feels like they truly belong.

'Inclusion is not a matter of political correctness. It is the key to growth.' – Jesse Jackson

8.

Rocky Road of Empowerment

In the shadows where potential hides,
A leader's fear, the tide abides.
With whispered doubts, we tend to stall,
Yet every voice can rise, can call.
To lift each other, break the chain,
In shared empowerment, we all gain.

The greatest gift you can give someone is your own personal development. I used to say, 'If you will help me, I will help you.' Now I say, 'I will help you, and you will help me. – Jim Rohn

In a world where collaboration drives innovation, empowering others has emerged as the heartbeat of successful workplaces.

Picture a team buzzing with enthusiasm, creativity, and confidence, where every voice matters and every idea is celebrated. But despite its undeniable benefits, many leaders find themselves grappling with the challenges of true Empowerment.

Why does this happen? Let's uncover the hurdles, share personal stories, and unlock the transformative power of Empowerment in the workplace!

The Essence of Empowerment in the Workplace

When we talk about Empowerment, we essentially refer to giving individuals the tools, resources, and confidence they need to take ownership of their work and make informed decisions. It's about creating an environment where team members feel supported enough to express their ideas, take risks, and grow professionally. In a nutshell, Empowerment is about trust, Autonomy, and development.

What Does Empowerment Look Like?

Empowerment can take various forms in the workplace, including:

1. **Delegation of Authority:** Allowing team members to make decisions in their areas of responsibility.
2. **Encouragement of Initiative:** Motivating colleagues to propose new ideas and solutions without Fear of criticism.
3. **Providing Resources:** Offering training, mentorship, or tools that facilitate professional growth.
4. **Creating a Safe Space for Failure:** Cultivating an environment where mistakes are viewed as learning opportunities rather than failures.

However, despite the clear benefits of Empowerment, it can feel like an uphill battle for many reasons.

The Hurdles We Face in Empowering Others

1. Fear of Losing Control

One of the primary barriers to Empowerment is Fear of losing control over the work process, fear that mistakes will occur, or even fear that someone might outshine us. It's human nature to want to maintain a certain level of authority, especially in a professional setting. This Fear can lead to micromanagement, which ultimately stifles growth and innovation.

2. Lack of Communication

Another significant hurdle is the lack of effective Communication. Sometimes, we operate under the assumption that our colleagues understand their roles and responsibilities without needing clear instructions. This can lead to confusion and frustration, ultimately hampering empowerment efforts. When we fail to articulate our expectations and objectives, we inadvertently limit others' ability to contribute meaningfully.

3. Time Constraints

The fast-paced nature of many workplaces can also hinder Empowerment. When we are swamped with our tasks, it's easy to overlook opportunities to support our colleagues. We may think we are helpful by taking on more responsibilities rather than giving others the chance to grow.

4. Personal Insecurities

Our insecurities can also play a significant role. We may worry that empowering others will expose our own weaknesses or make us seem less competent. This can lead to a reluctance to delegate tasks or responsibilities, ultimately hindering both our growth and that of our colleagues.

5. Resistance to Change

Finally, some individuals or teams may be resistant to change. If a workplace has traditionally operated hierarchically, shifting to a more empowering, collaborative approach can be met with skepticism. Team members might feel comfortable with the status quo and unwilling to embrace new working methods.

My Journey with Empowerment

Let me illustrate the hurdles of Empowerment from my experience.

A few years ago, I was on a project team responsible for launching a new project. We were all excited, and I was particularly enthusiastic about mentoring a junior team member, Anupama. She was bright, eager to learn, and had some fantastic ideas.

The Beginning of a Journey

From the outset, I saw a lot of potential in Anupama. She was passionate about the project and had fresh ideas that I felt could add real value. I was excited about helping her develop her skills and confidence. But as we started working together, I began to feel the pressure of the project deadlines.

Slipping into Micromanagement

As the project progressed, I was slipping into the habit of micromanaging her. I believed my experience was necessary to guide her effectively, so I often took over tasks instead of letting her handle them. The rationale in my mind was clear. I didn't want to risk any mistakes that could derail our timeline. In doing so, I thought I was being a responsible team leader.

But the reality was starkly different. My desire to maintain control led me to stifle Anupama's creativity and confidence. Instead of empowering her to take ownership, I told her I didn't trust her abilities. The irony wasn't lost on me. I wanted to uplift her, yet my actions did the opposite.

The Wake-Up Call

As we approached the project deadline, I began to feel overwhelmed. I had taken on so much of the work that I was burning out, which led to stress and anxiety. Meanwhile, Anupama was sitting there, feeling unmotivated and undervalued. I could see it in her demeanor. She was no longer the enthusiastic team member I had initially recognized.

One day, during a team meeting, I was discussing the progress we had made. As I spoke, I glanced at Anupama and saw a flicker of disappointment in her eyes. That moment was my wake-up call. I realized that by not empowering her, I had stifled her growth and placed an unnecessary burden on myself.

Taking a Step Back

That evening, I did some serious reflection. I understood that Empowerment isn't just a style word. It's a crucial aspect of effective leadership. I needed to step back and allow Anupama to take charge of specific aspects of the project.

The next day, I approached her with a different mindset. I explained my concerns and acknowledged my mistake in trying to take over. I emphasized that I believed in her abilities and wanted her to lead a segment of the project.

The Transformation

When I finally allowed Anupama to take charge, everything changed. I gave her the Autonomy to make decisions and approach tasks independently. I clarified that I was there for support and guidance, but she was in the driver's seat.

To my delight, Anupama flourished. She approached her responsibilities with newfound energy and creativity. Her confidence soared as she started making decisions and offering innovative ideas. The project transformed into a collaborative effort where we contributed significantly, each playing to our strengths.

The Successful Outcome

As a result of this shift in dynamics, we completed the project on time, and the product launch was a success –

largely thanks to Anupama's contributions. The entire experience taught me valuable lessons about Empowerment. It's not just about delegation but about trust, collaboration, and creating an environment where everyone can thrive.

The Broader Impact of Empowerment

Empowering others can significantly impact team dynamics and overall workplace culture. Here are a few key benefits that stem from a culture of Empowerment –

1. Enhanced Morale

When team members feel empowered, their morale often improves. They feel valued and recognized for their contributions, leading to increased job satisfaction. A positive workplace culture fosters loyalty and commitment, reducing turnover rates and attracting top talent.

2. Improved Collaboration

Empowerment encourages open Communication and collaboration. Team members are likelier to share their ideas and engage in discussions, leading to innovative solutions and enhanced team dynamics. A collaborative culture promotes a sense of belonging, where everyone feels they have a stake in the team's success.

3. Increased Productivity

When empowered, individuals are more motivated to take ownership of their work. This often leads to higher levels of productivity. Empowered employees are likelier to go above and beyond, striving to achieve individual and team goals.

4. Development of Future Leaders

Empowering others also plays a crucial role in developing future leaders. When team members can take on responsibilities and make decisions, they gain valuable experience that prepares them for leadership roles. This is essential for succession planning and ensuring the long-term success of an organization.

5. A Culture of Learning

Finally, an empowered workplace fosters a culture of learning and growth. When mistakes are seen as opportunities for improvement rather than failures, employees feel encouraged to take risks and try new things. This mindset leads to continuous development and innovation, benefiting both the individual and the organization.

Strategies for Effective Empowerment

So, how can we empower our colleagues more effectively? Here are some practical strategies to consider:

1. Communicate Clearly and Openly

Effective Communication is the cornerstone of Empowerment. Don't assume that your colleagues know what to do. Take the time to explain your vision, outline expectations, and clarify their roles within the team. Encourage open dialogue where team members feel comfortable asking questions and sharing their ideas.

2. Provide Necessary Resources

Ensure your team members have access to the resources they need to succeed. This could include training, mentorship, or tools that facilitate their professional growth. Investing in your team sends a powerful message that you are committed to their development.

3. Encourage Autonomy

Allow team members to make decisions and take ownership of their projects. Please resist the urge to micromanage – give them the space to find their way. This boosts their confidence and fosters a sense of responsibility and accountability.

4. Celebrate Contributions

Recognize and celebrate the successes of your colleagues. Acknowledgment can take many forms, from a simple thank-you email to a shout-out in a team meeting. Celebrating contributions fosters a culture of appreciation and motivates others to excel.

5. Foster an Open Environment

Create a culture where it's okay to share ideas and feedback. Encourage questions and discussions to ensure everyone feels included. An open environment promotes creativity and innovation, empowering individuals to express themselves.

6. Provide Constructive Feedback

Feedback is a crucial aspect of Empowerment. Offer constructive feedback that helps individuals grow and develop. Make it a point to focus on strengths while providing guidance for improvement. This balanced approach builds trust and encourages a growth mindset.

7. Lead by Example

As a leader, your behavior sets the tone for the team. Demonstrate Empowerment by actively involving team members in decision-making and valuing their input. When you model empowered behavior, you create a ripple effect that encourages others to follow suit.

Overcoming the Barriers

While the strategies above are essential for effective Empowerment, addressing the barriers hindering these efforts is crucial. Here are some ways to overcome common obstacles –

1. Addressing Fear

To combat the Fear of losing control, focus on building trust within your team. Share your experiences and vulnerabilities, and encourage open conversations about concerns. When team members feel safe expressing their fears, empowering them becomes more manageable.

2. Enhancing Communication

Improve Communication by regularly checking in with your team. Schedule one-on-one meetings to discuss their progress and address any challenges they may be facing. Foster an environment where feedback is a two-way street, allowing continuous improvement.

3. Prioritizing Empowerment

Make Empowerment a priority in your team's goals. Allocate time during team meetings to discuss empowerment strategies and encourage team members to share their ideas. When Empowerment is ingrained in the team's culture, it becomes a natural part of the workflow.

4. Fostering a Growth Mindset

Encourage a growth mindset within your team. Emphasize that mistakes are learning opportunities and that taking risks is essential for growth. Celebrate efforts, not just results, to create an environment where individuals feel comfortable trying new things.

5. Continuous Learning and Development

Invest in training and development programs that focus on empowerment and leadership skills. Encourage team members to participate in workshops or courses that help them build their confidence and abilities. Continuous learning fosters a culture of growth and prepares individuals for future challenges.

Embracing the Challenge of Empowerment

Empowering others may sometimes feel like a daunting task, especially when we are juggling our responsibilities. But remember, it's not about relinquishing control but sharing it. Allowing others to step up creates a more dynamic workplace where everyone can thrive.

So, the next time you are faced with the opportunity to empower a colleague, take a deep breath, trust your instincts, and let them shine. You might just be surprised by the positive outcomes – not only for them but also for you and your entire team.

I encourage you to embrace the challenge of Empowerment. It may be a hurdle, but it can become a stepping stone to success with the right mindset and strategies.

Together, let's create workplaces where Empowerment is not just a concept but a lived reality.

Let's uplift one another and pave the way for growth, innovation, and collective achievement. After all, when we empower others, we empower ourselves, which is a win-win for everyone involved.

'Empowerment is the ability to be truly who you are and to give others the freedom to be who they are.' – Sheryl Sandberg

9.

Cultivating a Supportive Environment

In the heart of the office, a challenge takes flight,
Where shadows of doubt dim the brightest light.
Yet kindness can blossom, and trust can arise,
When we lift each other, like stars in the skies.
Together we flourish, with voices that blend,
Cultivating a space where all hearts can mend.

'A toxic workplace will drain even the brightest talent, while a supportive environment allows everyone to shine.'

Workplaces are where we spend a considerable chunk of our time. Yet, despite all the time and energy we pour into our work, one of the most common hurdles we face is the lack of a supportive environment.

I have experienced this firsthand, and I will share a personal story to show how much of a difference it can make.

But first, let's get into what a Supportive Environment really means. Why does it matter, and how can we create one?

What is a Supportive Environment?

An environment where employees feel valued, heard, and empowered to do their best work. It's where people trust each other, communicate openly, and feel comfortable being themselves.

In a supportive environment, challenges are met with solutions, not judgment. Conflicts are handled with respect, and failures are seen as learning opportunities.

When we talk about cultivating this kind of environment, we are really talking about creating a space where people want to show up, not just because they have to pay the bills, but because they genuinely feel good about being there. It's about fostering an atmosphere where collaboration is natural, not forced, and people think they are part of something meaningful.

Why is it Important

We all know how much stress can drag us down. A toxic work environment can make even the most talented, dedicated employee lose motivation. When there is tension, when people do not feel supported, productivity drops, communication breaks down, and, ultimately, people start leaving. And let's be honest – good employees are hard to come by and even harder to replace.

In contrast, a supportive environment boosts morale, helps teams work better together, and leads to higher job satisfaction. It's not just about making work *'feel nice'* or having a positive vibe. A supportive environment directly impacts the company's success. The happier and more engaged the team, the better the results.

A Tale of Two Workplaces

Let me share two experiences so you understand how much the workplace environment matters. The difference wasn't just in how things were handled on the surface, it was in the mindset, the culture, and how my colleagues and I were treated daily.

Workplace 1: The Stress Factory

The first workplace that left me drained and demoralized. From the outside, it might have looked like a high-performing, fast-paced company with much ambition. But beneath that glossy exterior was a culture of fear and competition.

The Communication Void

In this environment, communication was either nonexistent or downright hostile. There were hardly any team meetings, and when there were, they were dominated by senior leadership, who made it clear that we were there to follow orders, not to contribute ideas. Feedback was top-down, often delivered with sharp criticism, and rarely constructive. When something went wrong, it wasn't discussed in a way that would lead to improvement. Instead, fingers were pointed, and people were blamed – usually publicly.

I remember once making a mistake on a report used in a client presentation. It wasn't a huge mistake, but it wasn't perfect. My manager didn't pull me aside to discuss or ask me what happened. Instead, I was called out during a team meeting in front of everyone. The feedback wasn't, *'Here's how we can avoid this in the future,'* but more along the lines of, *'How could you let this happen?'* I left that meeting feeling embarrassed and anxious, knowing that everyone around me probably thought, *'Glad that wasn't me.'*

The Fear Culture

People weren't encouraged to take risks or think creatively. In fact, doing so could backfire. I quickly learned that it was safer to stay quiet, keep my head down, and stick to the status quo. There was an overwhelming sense that mistakes would be punished, not learned from.

For example, I had many ideas for how to streamline processes and make things more efficient. But every time I thought about bringing it up, I hesitated. I had seen others try to suggest improvements only to be shot down. The leadership wasn't interested in change unless it was their idea, and even then, they rarely consulted with the people who were actually doing the work. It created this bizarre paradox where we all worked harder than necessary. Still, no one felt empowered to say anything about it.

Isolation and Competition

To make matters worse, the company thrived on internal competition. Promotions and rewards were given to the cutthroat, not necessarily the most collaborative or innovative. People were pitted against each other, fostering a mistrustful culture.

I remember overhearing coworkers talk about how they didn't want to help someone on a project because it might mean that person would get ahead of them.

This wasn't just occasional. It was ingrained in the fabric of the workplace. Teamwork was practically nonexistent. Even though we were all technically working towards the same goals, it felt like everyone was out for themselves.

And because of that, we weren't sharing knowledge, we weren't learning from each other, and we certainly weren't supporting one another. It was exhausting.

The Toll on Well-Being

After a few months, the anxiety started affecting me beyond the office. I was constantly worried about making mistakes. I would double and triple-check every small task, fearing the consequences of something slipping through the cracks. It got to the point where Sunday evenings would fill me with dread because I knew I had to face another week of stress and blame.

I remember staying late at the office, not because I had that much work to do but because I was afraid that leaving on time would make me look less committed. People regularly sent emails after midnight to signal how dedicated they were. It was as if working yourself to the bone was some badge of honor. But in reality, it was a fast track to burnout.

I knew I couldn't sustain this pace forever. My productivity suffered, not because I wasn't capable, but because I was constantly working in fear and stress.

And the worst part? I wasn't alone. My coworkers were going through the same struggles, but we didn't have the kind of environment where we could talk about it. Everyone was trying to survive.

Workplace 2: The Empowerment Zone

My next job was a complete 180.

This second workplace wasn't perfect (no workplace is). Still, it was everything the first one wasn't – it was supportive, collaborative, and growth-oriented. And from the moment I joined, I could feel the difference.

The Open-Door Culture

One of the first things I noticed was how open the communication was. Unlike my previous job, where leadership was distant and unapproachable, managers made it clear that they wanted to hear from everyone, regardless of rank. They encouraged us to share our ideas, whether rough or unfinished. Mistakes weren't punished, they were seen as part of the process.

For instance, in my first month, I was working on a big project and felt unsure about a decision I had to make. Instead of hiding my uncertainty (like I had in the first job), I went to my manager. Rather than dismissing my concerns, she sat with me and helped me think through it. I left that conversation with an answer and a new level of confidence in my decision-making skills.

Collaboration Over Competition

Collaboration was the name of the game here. Instead of competing, we were encouraged to work together and share knowledge. Teamwork wasn't just lip service, it was baked into how we operated. We had regular team check-ins where everyone was encouraged to share updates, challenges, and personal wins.

One time, I was struggling to meet a deadline on a report. Instead of leaving me to sink, a coworker offered to help me with some data analysis. He didn't do it for recognition or because he would get anything out of it – he just knew I needed a hand, and that's what teammates did for each other. In return, when he needed some help with a presentation a few weeks later, I jumped in to support him.

This kind of mutual aid was standard practice, not the exception.

A Culture of Feedback and Growth

The feedback culture in this second job was radically different. Instead of avoiding feedback because it was tied to shame or punishment, I looked forward to it. Regular one-on-ones with my manager weren't dreaded performance reviews – they were conversations about how I could continue to grow. Even when I made mistakes, the focus was always on improving, not assigning blame.

I distinctly remember one presentation I gave that didn't go as planned. I was nervous, stumbled through parts of it, and generally felt I hadn't delivered at my best. Afterward, I braced myself for the criticism I had received in my previous job. Instead, my manager asked, *'What do you think went well, and what do you want to work on next time?'* It was a simple shift in approach, but it changed everything. He wasn't there to tear me down but to help me get better. And because of that, I left that meeting feeling motivated, not defeated.

Well-Being and Balance

This second workplace also prioritized well-being in ways the first never had. The company actively encouraged us to take time off, not just when sick but to prevent burnout. If someone seemed overwhelmed, their workload was adjusted. It was understood that we weren't machines and that taking care of ourselves meant we could do our best work.

There was no pressure to work late to prove our commitment. We would stay and get the job done if we had a deadline.

But there was no unhealthy expectation of constant availability. People respected boundaries. I felt a balance between my work and personal life, which had been completely missing at the first job.

The Result: Thriving vs. Surviving

The difference between these two environments was night and day. In the first job, I was surviving – barely getting through each day, constantly stressed, and always waiting for the next shoe to drop. I was physically there, but mentally, I had checked out long before I left the company.

In the second job, I thrived. I was engaged, motivated and genuinely looked forward to coming to work each day. I felt supported and heard, and because of that, I could do my best work.

It wasn't the work that made the difference, it was the environment. The way people communicated, the level of trust, and the emphasis on collaboration rather than competition were the things that turned a job into a place where I could thrive.

The Key Ingredients of a Supportive Environment

So, what makes a workplace genuinely supportive? Let's break down the core elements that can make or break this kind of atmosphere:

1. Open Communication

People need to feel they can speak up without fear of judgment. Whether offering feedback, asking for help, or sharing new ideas, communication must flow both top-down and bottom-up. Leadership should encourage an open-door policy, ensuring that all voices matter, not just those with seniority.

2. Empathy

A supportive environment isn't just about getting the work done. It's about understanding the people doing it. Empathy means recognizing that your employees are human, with emotions, challenges, and lives outside the office. It means being flexible when someone needs a mental health day or allowing them to learn from their mistakes without immediately penalizing them.

3. Teamwork

Collaboration should be encouraged, not competition. When employees feel like there are working with each other rather than against each other, much more gets done. Create opportunities for team-building and collective problem-solving. Make sure individual achievements are celebrated and emphasize the importance of collective success.

4. Feedback Culture

Constructive feedback is one of the most valuable tools in the workplace, but it needs to be delivered correctly. It should be timely, specific, and aimed at helping the person grow. Regular check-ins can prevent minor issues from becoming more significant problems, and more importantly, they can be an opportunity to celebrate progress and address concerns before they escalate.

5. Psychological Safety

People need to know they can take risks, make mistakes, and be themselves without fear of punishment or ridicule. This is critical for innovation. The company will stagnate if employees are too afraid to speak up or suggest new ideas because they fear backlash.

6. Support Systems

This goes beyond emotional support. Companies need to provide the right tools, resources, and development opportunities so employees can grow in their roles. Whether investing in professional development or ensuring employees have the right software and training, giving people what they need to succeed is crucial to building a supportive environment.

What You Can Do as an Employee

Even if you are not in a leadership position, you can still help create a supportive environment around you. Here are some small ways you can contribute:

- **Be the Listener:** When a colleague needs to vent or share an idea, be there to listen without judgment. Sometimes, just having someone hear you can make all the difference.
- **Offer Help:** If you see someone struggling, don't wait for them to ask for help. Offer it. Even something as simple as asking, *'Is there anything I can do to make your day easier?'* goes a long way.
- **Celebrate Wins:** Take a moment to acknowledge the hard work of others. Whether it's a public shout-out or a private note, showing appreciation for your coworkers helps create a positive atmosphere.

Final Thoughts

Cultivating a supportive environment is one of the most important investments any workplace can make. It affects everything from employee morale to productivity to turnover rates. More than that, it creates a space where people feel they belong, can contribute their best ideas, and are excited to grow.

Looking back at my own experiences, the impact of a supportive environment – or the lack of one – couldn't be more obvious. It's not just about perks or surface-level policies. It's about creating a culture of respect, empathy, and collaboration, where everyone feels like there are a part of something bigger.

And whether you are a manager, a new hire, or somewhere in between, you have a role to play in cultivating that environment. When we feel supported, we do our best work, and that's when the magic happens.

'In the end, it's not just the work we do that defines our success, but the environment in which we do it.'

10.

Resilience and Mental Wellbeing

In the hustle of days where pressures collide,
We find strength within, a deep well inside.
When storms of stress gather, and shadows loom tall,
Resilience whispers softly, 'You can rise from the fall.'
With every setback, we learn to embrace,
The art of wellbeing, our steadying grace.

'Strength doesn't come from what you can do it comes from overcoming the things you once thought you couldn't.' – Rikki Rogers

When we talk about resilience and mental well-being in the workplace, we are diving into a space that most of us have experienced but perhaps not given enough thought to.

We often face moments at work that leave us feeling drained, stressed, or overwhelmed. But here is the thing – resilience is that invisible muscle we all have. It helps us bounce back from these challenges, stay mentally strong, and find balance despite the chaos. It's not about avoiding stress – it's about learning how to thrive in the middle of it.

What is Resilience?

Resilience is often misunderstood. Some people think it means being unbreakable or unaffected by problems. In reality, resilience is about being flexible and adaptable in adversity. It's your ability to recover from setbacks, adapt to change, and keep moving forward despite the difficulties.

Think of it as a rubber band. You stretch it, sometimes beyond its limit, but with the proper care, it always returns to its original shape. Resilience is the capacity of humans to *'stretch'* without breaking when life throws curveballs, especially in the workplace.

Mental Well-being at Work: Why It Matters

Mental well-being is more than just the absence of mental health issues like anxiety or depression. It's about how we feel, think, and function daily. It's having a sense of purpose, feeling confident, staying focused, and maintaining healthy relationships with colleagues. Our work environment plays a massive role in this.

Workplace stress is often inevitable. There are deadlines, tough conversations, decisions that don't always go your way, and a never-ending list of tasks. But when our mental well-being is compromised, even the most minor challenges can feel like mountains. That's why cultivating resilience is so important. It's not just about surviving the workday – it's about thriving, no matter what comes your way.

The Impact of Workplace Challenges

Let me share a real-life example from my own career that reflects how crucial resilience and mental well-being are. I worked in a fast-paced environment a few years ago where everything seemed on fire. There was constant pressure to deliver results, and I felt like I was barely keeping my head above water. Each day brought a new crisis – a project was going sideways, a client was unhappy, or an unforeseen issue with a team member. It was relentless.

At first, I could handle it by pushing harder, working longer hours, and sacrificing my time. Slowly, I began noticing the signs of burnout. I was always exhausted, had trouble sleeping, and was irritable even with people outside of work. It felt like my brain was in overdrive, constantly thinking about what I needed to do next.

One day, it all came to a head. I had been working on a major project for weeks, but it fell apart because of a last-minute change in the client's requirements. I had done everything possible to make it a success, but the situation was out of my control. And yet, I felt like a failure. I remember sitting at my desk, feeling ultimately defeated. For the first time in my career, I thought about quitting.

My Resilience

At that moment, I realized something had to change – not just in my workload but in how I approached my mental well-being. My mentor said, *'You cannot control every aspect of your job, but you can control how you respond to it.'* So, I started making a conscious effort to begin prioritizing my mental health.

1. **Setting Boundaries**

   The first thing I do is set better boundaries. I stopped checking emails late at night, creating a clear division between my work and personal life. That allowed me to mentally recharge outside of work.

2. **Seeking Support**

   I also leaned on my colleagues. In the past, I felt like I had to do everything myself. But I learned that asking for help isn't a weakness – it's a strength. By sharing the load with my team, we could all perform better.

3. **Changing My Mindset**

I had to shift from perfection to focusing on progress. Mistakes would happen, and some things would be out of my control. Instead of beating myself up, I started viewing setbacks as learning opportunities.

4. **Taking Care of My Body and Mind**

I made physical activity and mindfulness practices part of my routine. Whether going for a walk or practicing meditation, these small acts significantly reduced stress and improved my resilience.

Over time, I noticed a real change. I still faced challenges – those didn't go away – but my ability to handle them improved dramatically. Instead of spiraling when things went wrong, I could stay grounded, think clearly, and bounce back more quickly.

Practical Strategies to Build Resilience at Work

There are a few simple strategies you can start implementing today –

1. **Recognize the Signs of Stress Early**

Don't wait until burnout takes over. Pay attention to how you feel – mentally, physically, and emotionally. If you feel overwhelmed, take a step back and assess what is contributing to it.

2. Focus on What You Can Control

In any stressful situation, there will always be a few things that are outside of your control. Focus on the things you can influence, and let go of the rest. This mindset shift is critical to reducing unnecessary stress.

3. Develop a Support System

Whether it's colleagues, friends, or family, having people you can talk to when work gets tough is crucial. Sometimes, just talking things out can help you gain a new perspective and feel less isolated.

4. Practice Self-Compassion

Be kind to yourself, especially when things are unplanned. Perfection isn't the goal – progress is. Treat yourself with the same kindness and understanding that you would offer a friend.

5. Cultivate a Growth Mindset

Resilient people view setbacks as opportunities for growth. If something goes wrong, ask yourself: What can I learn from this experience? How can I use this challenge to become better at what I do?

6. Take Time to Recharge

Make sure you take time outside of work. Whether it's exercise, a hobby, or just relaxing with a good book, recharging is essential for maintaining resilience.

Why This Matters for You

Resilience and mental well-being are not just style words. They are essential components of a successful and fulfilling career. The more resilient you are, the better equipped you will be to handle the challenges that inevitably come your way at work. By prioritizing your mental well-being, you will improve your quality of life and be a better team member, leader, and overall contributor to your workplace.

You don't need to wait until you hit a breaking point like I did. Start building your resilience now, and make your mental well-being a priority. It's not just about getting through the tough times – it's about thriving in the face of them. And trust me, when you focus on resilience and mental health, you will notice the difference in your work and your entire life.

'Resilience isn't about avoiding the storms of life, but learning how to dance in the rain. Prioritize your mental wellbeing, and you will find strength not just to survive the challenges, but to thrive beyond them.'

11.

Self-Reflection and Growth

In the rush of daily tasks,
We often forget to pause and ask,
Am I growing, am I stuck?
What lessons hide beneath the muck?
Through reflection's honest light,
We find the strength to rise and fight.

'Growth begins when we start to question our own assumptions, and self-reflection is the path that leads us to our greatest potential.'

Our discussion on mental well-being made it clear that caring for our mental health is crucial for thriving in our personal and professional lives.

Another essential component of nurturing that well-being is self-reflection and growth.

I have spoken about self-reflection earlier as well as it is not just a trendy concept, it is a **powerful tool** that can help us navigate the complexities of the workplace while fostering our personal development.

Why Self-Reflection Matters

So, what exactly is self-reflection? It is the practice of stepping back from our daily grind to evaluate our thoughts, feelings, and actions. It is like pausing in a fast-paced race to check your map and adjust your direction if necessary. In the hustle and bustle of the workplace, we often forget to check in with ourselves. However, self-reflection helps us understand our motivations, recognize our strengths and weaknesses, and ultimately guide our growth.

The Connection to Growth

Now, let's talk about growth.

Self-reflection isn't just a moment of contemplation. It is an active process that fuels our development. When we take the time to reflect, we create opportunities to learn from our good and bad experiences. This understanding allows us to set actionable goals, adapt our behaviors, and foster resilience in facing challenges.

Why Self-Reflection and Growth is a Workplace Challenge.

Despite its importance, self-reflection and growth can be significant challenges in the workplace. Here are a few reasons why:

1. **Fast-Paced Environment**

In today's work culture, where deadlines loom and tasks pile up, it's easy to get caught in a cycle of constant activity. Many of us are so busy *'doing'* that we forget to pause and reflect. This can lead to burnout, decreased motivation, and a lack of clear direction.

2. **Fear of Vulnerability**

Self-reflection often requires us to confront uncomfortable truths about ourselves–our weaknesses, mistakes, and areas for improvement. This can be daunting, especially in a competitive workplace where individuals may fear that admitting shortcomings could harm their reputation or career prospects.

3. **Lack of Support**

Not everyone works in a supportive environment that encourages self-reflection. Suppose leaders and colleagues don't prioritize Feedback or growth. In that case, it can create a culture where employees feel isolated in their struggles. Without a supportive network, the process of reflection can feel daunting and ineffective.

4. **Limited Time and Resources**

Many organizations don't allocate time or resources for personal development. Employees may feel pressured to prioritize immediate tasks over long-term growth, leading to a cycle of stagnation where self-reflection takes a backseat.

5. **Resistance to Change**

Change is often uncomfortable, and self-reflection can highlight the need for changes in habits, routines, or behaviors. This resistance can make it challenging to embrace growth opportunities, as people may cling to familiar patterns – even if they are not serving them well.

A Personal Story – Chaos into Growth

Let me take you back a few years to one of the most stressful moments of my career that nearly knocked me off balance but ultimately taught me the power of self-reflection. It was a high-stakes project, and I had been handed the reins to lead it. The task initially seemed straightforward – manage a team, meet the client's expectations, and deliver on time. I felt confident and ready to lead my team to success. But little did I know, I was steering straight into a storm.

The project started with promise. The team was excited, deadlines were ambitious but doable, and the client was clear about their vision. But as the weeks rolled on, things began to fall apart. One missed deadline became two. Then three. Communication among the team became fragmented, emails went unanswered, and tensions were starting to rise. I could sense the frustration bubbling beneath the surface but was too caught up in setting fires to address it. It felt like every day brought a new crisis, and my to-do list never stopped growing.

The stress began to take a toll. I stayed late at the office, glued to my laptop, trying to force solutions. I wasn't sleeping well, snapping at people over small things, and worst of all, I could feel the weight of failure pressing down on me. I had worked hard to get to this leadership role, and now it felt like I was drowning in it.

Instead of leading with calm, I led with urgency. I was short-tempered and rushed in meetings, pushing the team harder without taking the time to hear their concerns. I saw the anxiety on their faces, but I justified it with a *'tough leadership'* mindset. After all, we were in crisis mode, and things needed to get done. But no matter how much I pushed, nothing was getting fixed. The project was slipping through my fingers like sand, and I felt helpless to stop it.

Then came the turning point.

One evening, after another exhausting 12-hour day of spinning my wheels, I came home, sat at my kitchen table, and stared blankly at the wall. I felt like a failure – like I was letting everyone down: the team, the client, and myself. My mind was racing with thoughts of what went wrong, and for the first time, I realized I had no answers.

I knew something had to change but didn't know where to start.

In a moment of clarity, I grabbed a notebook and started writing down everything I could think of about the project. I let it all out – the frustrations, the stress, the missed deadlines, the team's struggles, and my own shortcomings. And as I wrote, patterns started to emerge.

Here is what I realized:

1. I had been so focused on the deliverables that I would have neglected entirely the people behind them.

2. My communication was reactive, not proactive. I had given instructions but not checked in with the team.

3. I made isolated decisions, assuming I had to carry the entire project.

4. Most importantly, I realized I hadn't truly listened to anyone – not my team, client, or myself.

That moment of reflection was like a gut punch, but it was also the wake-up call I desperately needed.

I could see clearly that my leadership had been rooted in ***panic, not purpose.*** I had been so consumed by the situation's urgency that I would forgotten the fundamental elements of leadership: communication, empathy, and trust.

Turning Reflection into Action

The next day, I walked into the office with a new mindset. Before doing anything, I called a team meeting. I could feel the tension in the room, and I knew this conversation wouldn't be easy. I took a deep breath and started with something I had rarely done before – admitting my mistakes.

'I have been reflecting on how things have been going,' I began, *'and I realize I haven't been the leader you all needed. I have pushed you hard without the support and communication necessary to succeed, and I am truly sorry.'*

The room was silent. For a second, I wondered if I had made things worse by showing vulnerability. But then, one of my team members spoke up. *'Thank you for saying that. We have been struggling, but knowing we are being heard feels good.'*

That moment changed everything. The floodgates opened, and my team began sharing their frustrations and concerns – things I had been too distracted to notice.

One person mentioned how they were unclear on their role within the project. Another pointed out how we were all working in silos, duplicating efforts instead of collaborating. A junior member of the team, who had been hesitant to speak up before, shared that they had ideas to streamline the workflow but didn't feel like there was space to contribute.

As I listened, I realized this wasn't just a project issue but a people issue. And it was my role as the leader to fix it.

The Road to Growth

With this newfound clarity, we took immediate steps to course-correct. We redefined team roles and responsibilities, created more transparent lines of communication, and set up daily check-ins to ensure everyone had a voice. But beyond the practical changes, something deeper shifted. The team felt heard, supported, and, most importantly, empowered. The atmosphere in the office transformed from one of tension to one of collaboration and trust.

For me, this was the actual moment of growth. It wasn't just about delivering the project – it was about learning how to lead in a way that fostered growth for everyone involved, myself included. I had always thought leadership was about having all the answers. Still, it's about asking the right questions, listening, and being open to change.

In the following weeks, we got the project back on track and completed it ahead of schedule. But more than that, we had built a stronger, more cohesive team that was willing to collaborate, innovate, and learn from mistakes. My leadership had shifted from one of control to one of trust, and that made all the difference.

What I Learned

Looking back, I realize that the chaos of that project was a blessing in disguise. It forced me to confront my flaws, step back, and reflect on how my actions impacted those around me. Self-reflection isn't easy – it requires honesty, vulnerability, and a willingness to change. But it's also among the most influential personal and professional growth tools.

This experience taught me that self-reflection isn't just about analyzing the past, it's about taking ownership of it and using those lessons to move forward. At that moment, when I sat at my kitchen table and scribbled down my thoughts, I wasn't just reflecting – I was planting the seeds for growth. And that growth not only improved my leadership but also created a healthier, more supportive environment for my entire team.

Final Thoughts

If there is one thing, I hope you take away from my story, self-reflection is not a sign of weakness – it's the key to unlocking your potential. It allows you to see yourself clearly, recognize where to improve, and give you the tools to do better next time. The workplace is full of challenges, but with self-reflection, each challenge becomes an opportunity for growth. And trust me, once you start embracing that process, you will be amazed at how much you and those around you can achieve.

'True growth happens not when we avoid our mistakes, but when we embrace them, reflect on them, and use them as stepping stones to become better versions of ourselves.'

12.

Conflict Resolution and Collaboration

In the workplace where ideas collide,
Voices clash, and egos often chide.
But through the storm, we find our way,
Listening close, we learn to sway.
Together we will build, create, and mend,
Turning conflict to strength, hand in hand, my friend.

'Collaboration allows us to know more than we are capable of knowing ourselves.' – Paul Solarz

Let's dive into a topic that, whether you like it or not, has probably crossed your path in the workplace: Conflict resolution and Collaboration.

It's one of those things that can either make or break a team and understanding how to navigate it can lead to a more harmonious work environment and better outcomes for everyone involved. So, grab a cup of coffee, get comfy, and discuss the ins and outs of resolving conflicts and fostering Collaboration.

Understanding the Nature of Conflict

Why conflicts arise in the workplace. We are all different, right? Different backgrounds, experiences, and perspectives shape how we see the world and approach our jobs. When you throw a group of people together, it's only natural that clashes will occur.

The Roots of Conflict

Conflicts can stem from various sources:

– **Different Communication Styles:** People communicate in unique ways. Some are straightforward, while others are more nuanced. For instance, you might have a colleague who prefers to get to the point. At the same time, another might appreciate a more diplomatic approach.

- **Diverging Goals:** In a work environment, team members often have individual goals that may not align perfectly with team objectives. This misalignment can lead to misunderstandings or feelings of being undervalued.
- **Resource Allocation:** Limited resources, whether budget, time, or staffing, can create tension. If two departments are vying for the same resources, conflicts can arise.
- **Personality Clashes:** Different personalities can sometimes rub each other the wrong way. A highly extroverted team member might clash with someone more reserved.

Understanding these roots is essential because it helps us approach Conflict with empathy rather than frustration.

A Campaign Conflict

As a young team member, I witnessed a campaign development meeting for a new project launch. Our team was diverse, combining creative thinkers and analytical minds. This diversity was our strength, but it also set the stage for Conflict.

One day, during a brainstorming session, one of our team members, Alex, presented a bold, outside-the-box concept that required a hefty budget. Alex was incredibly creative and had a ton of innovative ideas. On the other hand, we had Prabhakar, who was detail-oriented and focused on data and analytics. Prabhakar quickly shot down Alex's idea, citing financial risks and the need for more conservative strategies.

A heated debate ensued, with both sides adamant about their viewpoints. Tensions were high, and rather than collaborating, we were stuck in a cycle of blame and frustration. The atmosphere became so charged that some team members hesitated to contribute further, fearing being criticized.

Recognizing the Impact of Conflict

That experience taught me how crucial it is to recognize the impact of Conflict in a team setting. It wasn't just about Alex and Prabhakar disagreeing. It affected the entire team's morale and productivity. If my manager hadn't intervened, that Conflict could have festered, leading to resentment and, ultimately, a breakdown in teamwork.

When Conflict remains unresolved, it can lead to:

1. **Decreased Productivity:** Team members may spend more time worrying about interpersonal dynamics than focusing on their tasks.
2. **Low Morale:** A negative atmosphere can sap energy and enthusiasm, leading to disengagement.
3. **Turnover:** If Conflict becomes the norm and employees feel undervalued or unheard, they may seek opportunities elsewhere.

4. **Ineffective Collaboration:** Ongoing Conflict can hinder Collaboration, as team members may become unwilling to work together or share ideas.

Strategies for Effective Conflict Resolution

So, how do we tackle conflicts like the one I just described? I have witnessed and deployed a few strategies that worked and can help you, too –

1. Stay Calm and Collected

Emotions run high during conflicts. It's essential to keep a level head. When I stepped in, I took a deep breath, acknowledged the feelings on both sides and reminded everyone that our common goal was to deliver a successful campaign. Staying calm helps create an environment conducive to open dialogue.

Tip: If you feel emotional during a disagreement, take a moment to breathe deeply. This can help you regain your composure and approach the situation more rationally.

2. Practice Active Listening

This is a big one. Encourage team members to express their thoughts and feelings without interruption. In our case, I facilitated a round where each person could share their perspective without being cut off. This helped to ensure everyone felt heard and valued.

Active listening involves –

- **Paraphrasing:** Repeat back what you have heard to confirm understanding. For example, *'So I am hearing you are concerned about the budget constraints.'*
- **Empathizing:** Acknowledge the emotions involved. *'I can see that you are feeling frustrated by the constraints we are working under.'*
- **Clarifying:** If something isn't clear, ask questions. *'Can you elaborate on that point?'*

3. Identify Common Ground

Look for shared interests or goals. In our situation, we all wanted a successful marketing campaign. I guided the discussion back to that goal, prompting the team to think about how they could blend creativity with data-driven decisions.

Finding common ground can help shift the focus from what divides us to what unites us. This not only fosters Collaboration but also strengthens team bonds.

4. Collaborative Problem-Solving

Once everyone has shared their viewpoints, brainstorm solutions together. We began to explore ways to tweak Alex's creative idea to align it with the budget Prabhakar was concerned about. The team devised a revised, innovative, and financially feasible concept by working together.

Collaborative problem-solving involves –

- **Encouraging Creativity:** Allow team members to think outside the box initially without the constraints of budget or feasibility.
- **Evaluating Options:** Once ideas are on the table, evaluate them collectively. Which ideas resonate with the team? What compromises can be made?
- **Creating a Plan:** Once a solution is agreed upon, outline the steps needed to implement it. Assign responsibilities to ensure everyone is clear on their roles.

5. Follow Up

After the Conflict has been resolved, it's essential to follow up and ensure everyone is still on the same page. I made it a point to check in with Alex and Prabhakar a week later to see how they felt about the resolution and whether there were lingering concerns.

Following up helps reinforce the resolution and shows team members that their feelings and opinions matter. It also creates a culture of accountability where everyone is encouraged to maintain open lines of communication.

Building a Collaborative Culture

To foster an environment where Collaboration thrives and conflicts are managed well, consider these tips:

1. Encourage Open Communication

Create a culture where team members feel safe expressing their thoughts and concerns. Regular check-ins and team-building activities can help build trust.

Suggestion: Implement regular team meetings where everyone can voice their opinions and share project updates. This can help prevent conflicts from escalating in the first place.

2. Provide Training

Offer workshops or training sessions on conflict resolution and effective communication. The more equipped your team is, the better they will handle conflicts when they arise.

Consider partnering with a facilitator who can guide your team through exercises to enhance communication skills and build rapport.

3. Lead by Example

As a leader or colleague, demonstrate how to handle conflicts gracefully. When others see you addressing issues calmly and respectfully, they will likely follow suit.

Tip: Share your own experiences with Conflict and resolution during team meetings. This transparency can create a more open environment where team members feel comfortable discussing their challenges.

4. **Recognize and Celebrate Collaboration**

Acknowledge and celebrate instances of successful Collaboration within your team. This recognition can motivate others to work together and foster a culture of cooperation.

Idea: Create a *'Collaborator of the Month'* award where team members nominate each other for successful teamwork. This can be a fun way to highlight positive interactions and build camaraderie.

The Role of Leadership in Conflict Resolution

Leadership plays a pivotal role in shaping the culture of conflict resolution and Collaboration within a team. As a leader, how you handle conflicts will set the tone for the rest of the team. Here are some additional strategies for leaders to consider:

1. **Model Vulnerability**

Don't be afraid to show vulnerability when conflicts arise. Acknowledge your own mistakes or misunderstandings. This can help create a safe space for others to express their feelings and perspectives.

2. Be Proactive

Please don't wait for conflicts to arise before addressing them. Regularly check in with your team members to gauge their feelings and frustrations. Being proactive can help identify potential issues before they escalate.

3. Create a Conflict Resolution Framework

Establish a clear framework for conflict resolution that everyone understands. This might include steps for addressing disagreements, escalation processes, and how to seek help from leadership if needed.

4. Foster a Growth Mindset

Encourage a growth mindset within your team, where challenges are viewed as opportunities for learning and development. This perspective can help reduce fear around Conflict and promote a more collaborative atmosphere.

The Long-Term Benefits of Effective Conflict Resolution

When conflicts are resolved effectively, it paves the way for Collaboration. The project team that faced the Conflict produced a campaign that exceeded our expectations. Alex and Prabhakar ended up learning from each other, with Alex incorporating more data into his creative processes and Prabhakar becoming more open to innovative ideas.

This experience taught me the value of blending different perspectives. Here are some long-term benefits of effective conflict resolution and Collaboration:

- **Increased Innovation:** When diverse perspectives are valued and integrated, teams are more likely to develop creative solutions and innovative ideas.
- **Enhanced Team Cohesion:** Successfully navigating conflicts can strengthen team bonds, leading to a more cohesive and supportive work environment.
- **Better Decision-Making:** Collaborative teams often make more informed decisions because they draw on broader insights and expertise.
- **Higher Employee Satisfaction:** When team members feel heard and valued, they are more likely to be satisfied with their work environment, leading to lower turnover rates.

Embracing Conflict as an Opportunity

Navigating Conflict and fostering Collaboration is a continuous journey. It's about building relationships, understanding each other's perspectives, and working towards common goals. Remember, Conflict doesn't have to be the enemy, it can lead to growth, innovation, and stronger teams when handled correctly.

So, the next time you find yourself amid a workplace dispute, embrace the challenge and use it as an opportunity to collaborate and create something unique together. After all, the most successful teams aren't those that never have conflicts, they are the ones that know how to navigate them with grace and effectiveness.

As you progress in your professional journey, carry these insights. Approach conflicts as opportunities for learning and growth, not just for yourself but for your entire team. You will be amazed at what you can achieve together when you foster a culture of Collaboration and respect.

Now, let's roll up our sleeves, put these strategies into practice, and turn our workplace conflicts into stepping stones for success!

'In the midst of chaos, there is also opportunity.' – Sun Tzu

13.

The Space Between

In the space between the rush and race,
Pause to breathe, find your quiet place.
The hurdles ahead aren't set in stone,
Shift your view, and see how you have grown.
A moment to think, a chance to reset,
Your greatest success may not have come yet.

'Obstacles are not stop signs, they are guidelines.' – Robert H. Schuller.

As you begin Chapter 13, you might feel a hesitation or sense of superstition. It's ingrained in many of us to avoid this number, to think of it as unlucky or ominous. But what if, instead of viewing it as a hurdle, we saw it as an opportunity? What if Chapter 13 wasn't a void but rather a space to pause and reflect?

Life, like the workplace, often presents challenges that seem bigger in our minds than they are in reality. Sometimes, the hurdles we struggle with aren't the ones on the track but the ones we create in our heads – fears, doubts, and assumptions about what might go wrong.

This chapter represents that pause, that mental space where we stop running from the obstacle and choose to look at it from another angle. It's an invitation to consider: What stories am I telling myself about my own limitations? What unseen beliefs might be holding me back?

Take a moment. Breathe.

This isn't the chapter to skip, but rather the one to reset your mindset. Chapter 13 in this book isn't unlucky – it's just a number – the challenges you face are not roadblocks but opportunities in disguise. With this pause, you are not only preparing to leap over the next hurdle but also seeing it for what it truly is: a step toward success.

The Power of Mindset

The way we interpret challenges, setbacks, and even 'bad luck' has an enormous impact on our ability to succeed. In many cases, it's not the obstacle itself that determines the outcome but how we choose to perceive it.

This is where the power of mindset comes into play.

A fixed mindset tells us that our abilities are static – either we have what it takes, or we don't. In this mindset, obstacles are seen as threats, confirming our worst fears about our limitations. In contrast, a growth mindset is the belief that we can develop our abilities, learn new skills, and grow from our challenges. With a growth mindset, hurdles aren't reasons to stop – there are opportunities to learn, adapt, and overcome.

When facing a difficult situation at work, it's easy to let fear or self-doubt creep in. We might tell ourselves, *'I am not good at this'*, or *'This is too much for me.'* But the truth is, these thoughts are only as powerful as the energy we give them. By shifting our perspective, we can turn fear into curiosity and limitations into learning experiences.

Cognitive Reframing: A Simple Shift with Powerful Results

One of the most effective tools for overcoming mental hurdles is cognitive reframing – choosing to see a situation differently. For example, if you are faced with a challenging task, rather than thinking, *'I am not equipped for this,'* reframe the thought. *'This is a chance to stretch my skills and grow.'* The facts of the situation haven't changed, but your mindset has, and that makes all the difference in how you approach the task.

Here's the truth, obstacles are inevitable, but how you view them is entirely up to you. You can see them as walls blocking your path, or you can see them as rungs on a ladder that bring you closer to your goals.

Applying the Mindset Shift

Consider your current challenges at work. Whether it's a demanding project, a difficult colleague, or a setback in your career, please take a moment to reflect on how you have been thinking about it. Are you viewing it as a fixed obstacle or an opportunity for growth?

The simple act of reframing – shifting from *'I can't'* to *'I will figure this out'* – can unlock new solutions, creative approaches, and renewed energy.

By embracing the power of mindset, you can transform even the most intimidating hurdles into stepping stones toward success.

So, as you move forward in this book and in your professional journey, remember this: the biggest obstacle may not be the challenge in front of you but how you choose to see it. And once you have shifted your mindset, there is no limit to what you can overcome.

13 Reflective Questions

Take this moment to pause, reflect, and dig deeper into your mindset with these 13 questions –

1. What current challenge in your professional life feels like an insurmountable hurdle? How might you reframe this challenge to see it as an opportunity for growth?
2. What limiting beliefs are holding you back from achieving your full potential at work? Are these beliefs based on facts or fears?
3. How do you typically respond when faced with unexpected obstacles? Can you identify any patterns in your reactions?
4. Is there a recent workplace situation where you defaulted to a fixed mindset? How could you apply a growth mindset in a similar future scenario?
5. What is one fear you have been avoiding in your career? How might embracing that fear instead of avoiding it create new possibilities?
6. Think of a time when you succeeded after initially doubting your ability. What mindset shift helped you achieve that success?
7. What language do you use when talking to yourself about difficult tasks? How can you make that internal dialogue more empowering?
8. What professional skills do you believe are *'fixed'* and cannot be improved? How might you approach developing those skills with a growth mindset?
9. How does fear of failure impact the risks you take at work? What would you do differently if you weren't afraid to fail?

10. Can you identify an area of your work life where you tend to avoid challenges? What small step can you take today to face that challenge head-on?

11. What workplace obstacle have you been viewing as permanent? How could you begin to see it as temporary and solvable?

12. Who in your professional life embodies a growth mindset, and what can you learn from them? How can their approach inspire a shift in your own thinking?

13. How would your work and career evolve if you consistently embraced a growth mindset? What changes would you start making today?

This chapter represents a pause, the challenges in your journey are not meant to stop you – they are moments to reflect, refocus, and rise stronger. Such pause assists you with a chance to elevate, for greater achievements ahead.

Every obstacle is an opportunity to reshape your path and grow beyond your perceived limits. By shifting your mindset and embracing the hurdles ahead, you transform them into stepping stones toward success.

'The only limits to your success are the ones you place on your own mind.' – Unknown.

14.

Empathy and Understanding

In the bustling office where silence can scream,
Empathy's light flickers, a forgotten dream.
Behind every struggle, a story untold,
A heart weighed by burdens, a spirit grown cold.
Let's bridge the divide with understanding and grace,
For together we rise when we share the same space.

'Empathy is about finding echoes of another person in yourself.' – Mohsin Hamid

In the heart of a bustling office, where the hum of computers and the clatter of keyboards created a chaotic symphony, something was brewing beneath the surface. Tension hung in the air like a thick fog. Amidst the whirlwind of deadlines and pressure, a silent storm was gathering – a storm that would forever change the dynamics of our team.

As the autumn leaves outside began their dramatic descent, I was caught in the whirlwind of an impending product launch, a moment that should have been exhilarating but felt more like an impending disaster. Our team had poured months of effort into this project, investing our souls into every detail. But one crucial member, Swapna, seemed to drift through the storm like a ghost, her spark extinguished, her focus shattered.

With each missed deadline, my frustration morphed into boiling resentment. I couldn't understand why Swapna was dragging us down. In my eyes, she was the anchor weighing us into a tumultuous sea while I was desperately swimming against the tide. I raged silently inside as I watched her stare blankly at her screen, oblivious to the weight of our collective responsibilities.

But as the winds of fate would have it, a revelation lurked just beyond the horizon. Little did I know that the key to unlocking our success – and my own growth – lay not in pushing her harder but in understanding the storm within her. When I finally peeled back the layers of my assumptions, I was confronted with a truth that shook me to my core – the power of empathy could either build us up or tear us apart.

Standing on the edge of this revelation, I realized that this was not just Swapna's struggle. It reflected a more significant issue that haunted workplaces everywhere. The unspoken challenges that each of us faces can create barriers to collaboration and understanding, making empathy an ideal and a necessity.

When our frustrations overshadow our ability to connect with colleagues, we risk creating a toxic environment where talent goes untapped and potential remains unfulfilled.

It became clear to me that recognizing and addressing these emotional landscapes would be crucial in transforming our team's dynamics. Empathy would serve as the bridge to understanding and the foundation for rebuilding our working relationships. Understanding the significance of empathy was the first step toward creating a more cohesive and productive workplace, and it was time to delve deeper into why it matters.

The Importance of Empathy

So, what exactly is empathy?

Simply put, it's the ability to put yourself in someone else's shoes to understand their feelings, thoughts, and perspectives. It's not just about feeling sorry for someone, it's about genuinely connecting with their experience and recognizing the validity of their emotions.

The Science Behind Empathy

Research shows empathy is not just a nice-to-have trait, it significantly impacts our workplace dynamics. According to studies conducted by neuroscientists, empathy activates specific regions in the brain that are responsible for emotional processing and social interaction. This means that we use our brains to foster connection and collaboration when we engage in empathetic behavior.

Why Empathy Matters in the Workplace

Empathy fosters better communication, collaboration, and conflict resolution in a workplace setting. Here's why it matters –

1. **Improved Communication**

   Empathy allows for more straightforward and compassionate communication. When we understand where others are coming from, we can respond in more constructive and supportive ways.

2. **Enhanced Teamwork**

   Teams that practice empathy are more likely to collaborate effectively. When team members feel understood, they are more willing to share their ideas and concerns, leading to more innovative solutions.

3. **Conflict Resolution**

   Conflicts are inevitable in any workplace, but empathy can help diffuse tension. When we take the time to understand the other person's perspective, it becomes easier to find common ground and resolve disputes amicably.

4. **Higher Employee Satisfaction**

Employees who feel understood are generally happier and more engaged. This leads to increased job satisfaction and retention rates.

5. **Better Leadership**

Leaders who demonstrate empathy create a culture of trust and respect. This not only motivates their teams but also encourages loyalty and productivity.

A Turning Point

Our project was barreling toward its launch date, and every minute counted. The stakes were high, and we were all under pressure to perform.

Among us was Swapna, a brilliant but often quiet team member. She was responsible for a critical component of our project, a task that required precision and creativity. But lately, Swapna seemed distracted. She missed deadlines, often staring blankly during meetings, lost in her thoughts, I could only guess.

Frustration bubbled within me as I watched the clock tick away our precious time. How could Swapna be so uncooperative at such a crucial moment? Didn't she realize the weight of our responsibilities?

As the project progressed, my annoyance grew. I would mutter about her lack of commitment, assuming she was slacking off. Conversations with colleagues echoed my sentiments, we all felt the pressure, and her seemingly lackadaisical attitude only added to the stress. It felt like I was carrying a heavy backpack up a steep hill. At the same time, Swapna strolled leisurely behind me, unaware of the burden I felt.

One afternoon, I overheard a hushed conversation between two coworkers. They were discussing Swapna's family – how her mother had recently been diagnosed with a serious illness. A wave of guilt crashed over me like a sudden storm. Here I was, frustrated with her lack of focus while she was juggling a heavy personal burden. The realization hit me hard like tons of bricks. I had been so caught up in my own frustrations that I had failed to recognize the silent battle she was fighting.

That evening, I couldn't shake the weight of my thoughts. I replayed our interactions in my mind, feeling a deep sense of regret. How had I not considered that her distractions might stem from something more profound? I knew I had to make it right.

The next day, I approached Swapna with a heavy heart. I found her sitting at her desk, staring blankly at her computer screen. *'Hey, can we talk?'* I asked, my voice tinged with uncertainty. She looked up, surprise flickering across her face.

We moved to a quieter corner of the office, and I took a deep breath. *'I just wanted to say that I am really sorry for how I have reacted to you over the past few weeks. I thought you were being uncooperative, but I didn't know what you were going through.'*

Her expression softened, and she looked away, blinking back tears. *'It's been really tough,'* she admitted. *'My mom has been in and out of the hospital, and I have been trying to juggle work and caring for her. Some days, it feels like I am drowning.'*

At that moment, the walls I had built around my frustration crumbled. I could finally see her for who she was – a dedicated team member facing overwhelming challenges. My heart ached for her. We talked more, sharing our fears, hopes, and the pressure of expectations at work and in our personal lives.

It was a cathartic exchange, one that opened the floodgates of understanding. I offered to help adjust her workload and take on more tasks so she could focus on her family without the stress of our looming deadlines. To my surprise, she accepted, a weight visibly lifted from her shoulders.

The shift in our dynamic was almost palpable. Swapna became more engaged in meetings, contributing ideas with renewed purpose. She wasn't just a teammate anymore. She was someone I respected and admired for her resilience. Together, we tackled our project with a newfound synergy that had been missing.

As the launch date approached, the energy in our team transformed. What was once a source of tension became a shared journey, with Swapna and I collaborating closely, each encouraging the other. On launch day, as the product went live, a sense of accomplishment washed over us like a warm wave.

This experience taught me that empathy isn't just a soft skill. It's a powerful tool for building connections and fostering collaboration. It opened my eyes to the importance of understanding the unspoken struggles of my colleagues, allowing us to support one another in meaningful ways.

Effects of Empathy

This experience taught me that empathy isn't just about individual relationships. It has varied effects throughout the entire workplace. When we practice empathy, we create an environment where others feel safe to share their challenges. This open communication can lead to innovative solutions and improved team dynamics.

For instance, imagine a workplace where everyone is encouraged to share their struggles without fear of judgment. Team members would become more supportive and engaged. They would feel valued and understood, which can translate into increased productivity and loyalty to the company.

The Cost of a Lack of Empathy

Conversely, lacking empathy in the workplace can lead to significant problems. Here are a few consequences that can arise when empathy is lacking:

1. **Increased Turnover**

   Employees who feel unsupported or misunderstood are likelier to leave their jobs. High turnover rates can be costly for companies financially and in terms of team morale.

2. **Poor Collaboration**

   Collaboration suffers when team members cannot understand each other's perspectives. This can lead to miscommunications, errors, and missed deadlines.

3. **Heightened Stress**

A lack of empathy can create a stressful work environment. Employees may feel isolated or unsupported, leading to burnout and decreased job satisfaction.

4. **Negative Workplace Culture**

A culture that doesn't prioritize empathy can become toxic. Employees may feel compelled to hide their struggles, which can breed resentment and hostility.

How to Cultivate Empathy in the Workplace

So, how can we foster this culture of empathy? Here are some practical tips to get you started:

1. **Active Listening**

When someone is speaking, really listen. Don't just wait for your turn to talk. Show genuine interest in their feelings and concerns. Nod, make eye contact, and ask follow-up questions to demonstrate you are engaged.

2. **Encourage Open Dialogue**

Create spaces where employees feel safe to express their feelings and concerns. This could be through regular check-ins, team-building exercises, or anonymous feedback systems.

3. **Lead by Example**

Model empathetic behavior if you are in a leadership role. Please share your own challenges and how you cope with them. When employees see their leaders being vulnerable and open, it encourages them to do the same.

4. **Provide Support**

Offer resources for mental health and wellness. Encourage employees to take breaks, seek help, and prioritize self-care.

5. **Celebrate Differences**

Recognize that everyone has unique experiences and backgrounds. Celebrate diversity and encourage team members to share their stories. This foster understanding and connection among colleagues.

Final Thoughts

Empathy is a vital component of a thriving workplace. It allows us to connect on a human level, fostering collaboration, creativity, and understanding.

My journey with Swapna taught me that behind every distraction, missed deadline, or frustrated colleague, a story may be waiting to be uncovered – one that could change how we view empathy in the workplace forever.

As we navigate the complexities of our professional lives, let's remember the power of empathy. It can transform our relationships, teams, and workplace culture. By embracing empathy, we enhance our work experience and contribute to a more compassionate and understanding world.

'The greatest gift of human beings is that we have the power of empathy.' – Meryl Streep

15.

Overcoming Imposter Syndrome

In shadows of doubt, we often hide,
Wearing masks of fear, we walk inside.
But strength lies not in perfect grace,
It's found in the courage we boldly embrace.
You have earned your place, your path is true,
The imposter fades when you believe in you.

'Success is not the absence of doubt, but the courage to push through it.'

'I can't believe they hired me.'

This thought echoed when I entered my new job's sleek, glass-fronted office. Surrounded by people who seemed to exude confidence and brilliance, I felt like an imposter, a fraud in an expensive suit.

The weight of expectation pressed down on my shoulders, and I wondered how long it would be before someone figured out, I didn't belong there.

The Illusion of Confidence

Imposter Syndrome often begins with that first spark of doubt. You might have earned a promotion, landed a dream job, or completed a challenging project. Instead of feeling elated, you are consumed by fear and anxiety. You worry that you have somehow deceived everyone into thinking you are capable, and deep down, you are terrified that they will soon uncover the truth.

What's more, this feeling isn't limited to a specific demographic. It can affect anyone, regardless of gender, age, or level of expertise. Studies show that up to 70% of people experience these feelings at some point in their careers.

So, let's delve deeper into this phenomenon, understand its impact, and how we can conquer it together.

What is Imposter Syndrome?

Imposter Syndrome refers to an internal experience of believing you are not as competent as others perceive you to be. It is characterized by self-doubt, inadequacy, and a persistent fear of being exposed as a fraud. Even after achieving milestones, those suffering from Imposter Syndrome attribute their Success to external factors, like luck or timing, rather than their hard work or talent.

This syndrome is often linked to perfectionism. You may set unreasonably high standards for yourself, leading to a cycle of anxiety and disappointment. When you inevitably fall short of these standards, the result can be an overwhelming sense of failure, reinforcing the belief that you are an imposter.

Wading Through Imposter Syndrome

On that Monday morning, as I walked through the office. I felt excitement and dread. Bursting with ambition and dreams, but the reality of my surroundings was both inspiring and intimidating. I noticed my new colleagues – each seemed to embody confidence. Some were engaged in lively discussions, while others were focused on their screens, their brows furrowed in concentration. Then there was me, an anxious newcomer who felt like a deer caught in headlights. I felt like I was playing dress-up in someone else's life.

My first major assignment was to lead a team meeting. My stomach churned as I was convinced, I wouldn't measure up. I stood before my colleagues, heart racing, palms clammy. Despite my preparation, I could feel my voice quivering.

'Today, I want to share our project status for the month that has gone by,' I began, but I could barely focus on my own words. All I could think was, *'what if I mess up? What if they see how clueless I really am?'*

As I presented, I noticed a few nods of approval. But instead of feeling relieved, I thought, they are just being polite. I received positive feedback when the meeting ended, yet I couldn't shake the feeling that it was all a façade. I thought *'if they only knew, I would barely have understood the project myself.'*

In the following weeks, I poured myself into my work, putting in extra hours to ensure I was *'good enough.'* I took on additional responsibilities and over-prepared for every meeting. Yet, despite my efforts, the feeling of inadequacy persisted. Each achievement felt like a fluke, a stroke of luck rather than a testament to my abilities.

One day, I found myself confiding in a mentor over coffee. *'I am so scared that one day, they will figure out I am just faking it,'* I admitted, my voice trembling. My mentor looked at me with understanding. *'You are not alone,'* she said. *'I have felt that way too. It's more common than you think.'* Hearing that even someone I admired had experienced similar feelings made me realize that I wasn't an isolated case.

Gradually, I began to confront my fears. I started to acknowledge my accomplishments rather than dismissing them. I kept a success journal where I recorded positive feedback and milestones. Whenever self-doubt crept in, I would flip through its pages and remind myself of the hard work that had gotten me to where I was.

Why Do We Feel This Way?

Imposter Syndrome is often deeply rooted in our upbringing and societal expectations. Many of us are conditioned to equate Success with constant achievement. This leads to the dangerous belief that we fail if we do not constantly excel.

Moreover, comparisons can trigger these feelings. In an era of social media, it's easy to scroll through curated highlights of others' lives and feel inadequate. But remember, you are only seeing a snapshot of someone else's journey – every story has its struggles.

Past experiences can also leave lasting scars. If you were often told to *'prove yourself'* or received harsh criticism, those messages can linger and shape your self-perception.

It's essential to recognize how these narratives affect your current mindset.

A few Strategies to Overcome Imposter Syndrome

Feeling overwhelmed by Imposter Syndrome? You are not alone, and there are actionable steps you can take to combat these feelings. Here's how –

1. Acknowledge Your Feelings

The first step in overcoming Imposter Syndrome is recognizing and accepting that you are experiencing these feelings. Acknowledgment is powerful. By naming it, you can start to understand it and diminish its control over you.

2. Reframe Your Thoughts

When negative self-talk arises, challenge those thoughts. Instead of telling yourself, *'I am not good enough,'* reframe it to, *'I bring unique skills to the table.'* This shift can help build a more positive self-image.

3. Celebrate Your Successes

Create a habit of celebrating your achievements, both big and small. Record positive feedback, completed projects, or even small victories. Reflecting on your successes can reinforce your sense of self-worth.

4. Seek Support

Don't hesitate to confide in trusted colleagues, mentors, or friends. Sharing your feelings can alleviate the burden and provide you with perspective. Often, you will find that others share similar experiences.

5. Set Realistic Goals

Instead of aiming for perfection, set achievable goals that allow for growth and learning. Break larger tasks into smaller, manageable steps to reduce feelings of overwhelm.

6. Embrace Mistakes

Recognize that mistakes are a natural part of the learning process. Instead of fearing failure, view it as an opportunity for growth. When I adopted this mindset, I found freedom in taking risks without the crippling fear of exposure.

7. Practice Self-Compassion

Treat yourself with the same kindness you would offer a friend. If you wouldn't criticize someone else for making a mistake, don't do it to yourself. Self-compassion can help ease feelings of inadequacy.

8. Visualize Success

Visualization can be a powerful tool. Picture yourself succeeding in a particular task, and imagine how it feels to achieve your goals. This technique can help boost your confidence and reduce anxiety.

Moving Forward

Overcoming Imposter Syndrome is a continuous journey. It requires patience, self-awareness, and a willingness to confront your doubts. Remember that you are not an imposter but a capable and talented individual who deserves Success.

As you move forward, keep in mind that everyone has their struggles. The next time you doubt yourself, remind yourself of your unique strengths and the journey that brought you here. Own your achievements and embrace your journey – every step, every misstep, and every triumph.

So, take a deep breath, stand tall, and recognize that you belong at the table. You have earned your place, and it's time to embrace your true self. You are not just surviving in your role, you are thriving – and you are well on your way to conquering Imposter Syndrome, one step at a time!

'You are not an imposter, you are simply someone who continues to grow and learn. Own your journey, and trust that you belong.'

16.

Mindfulness and Stress Management

In moments rushed, the mind will race,
But stillness finds its quiet place.
A breath, a pause, to slow the pace,
And stress begins to lose its trace.
In mindful calm, we learn to see,
The peace within sets us free.

'Mindfulness isn't difficult. What's difficult is to remember to be mindful.' – Jon Kabat-Zinn

Stress. We all experience it.

Stress is a constant companion in most workplaces today. Stress will always be present, whether juggling deadlines, managing a team, dealing with office politics, or simply staying afloat with your daily tasks.

But what if I told you there's a way to manage stress that doesn't involve leaving your job, taking long vacations, or some other major lifestyle overhaul? That's where mindfulness comes in.

What Is Mindfulness?

At its core, mindfulness is the practice of being fully present in the moment – acknowledging your thoughts, emotions, and sensations without getting caught up in them. It's about observing what's happening right now without judgment or overreaction.

Think of mindfulness like this – You are driving in traffic, and someone cuts you off. Your body tightens, your heart rate speeds up, and your mind instantly creates a narrative: *'How dare they? They are so reckless! I am going to be late now!'* It's easy to spiral from there, maybe carrying that stress throughout the day. But imagine if, in that moment, you paused and noticed your reaction. Instead of getting lost in the anger or frustration, you acknowledged it – *'I feel angry and tense right now'* – and then let it pass. That's mindfulness in action.

Why Is Stress So Common in the Workplace?

Before diving into how mindfulness can help, let's first look at why stress is a common workplace hurdle. The modern work environment is filled with triggers:

- **Pressure to perform:** Tight deadlines, high expectations from bosses, and fear of failure can create constant pressure.
- **Lack of control:** You may not have control over the tasks you are given or the pace at which you are expected to work, leading to frustration and helplessness.
- **Multitasking:** We are often expected to juggle multiple tasks simultaneously, but the truth is, our brains aren't designed for that. It splits our focus and adds to our stress.
- **Unclear communication:** Misunderstandings or unclear expectations can lead to confusion, rework, and tension.
- **Work-life balance**: With the lines between work and personal life often blurred, especially in remote work setups, it's easy to feel like you are never really off the clock.

How Mindfulness Can Help Manage Stress

The beauty of mindfulness is that it doesn't require hours of practice or a unique setting. In any situation, you can apply mindfulness techniques right in the middle of your workday. Here is how it helps –

1. Improves Focus

Mindfulness allows you to fully engage with the task at hand by bringing your attention to the present moment. When focused on one thing, you are less likely to feel overwhelmed by all the other things on your to-do list.

2. Reduces Reactivity

One of the biggest sources of stress is our reaction to external events. When you practice mindfulness, you learn to respond thoughtfully rather than react impulsively. You might still feel angry or frustrated, but instead of letting those feelings dictate your actions, you observe them, take a breath, and choose a more measured response.

3. Enhances Emotional Regulation

Mindfulness allows you to become more aware of your emotions without being swept away. This doesn't mean you ignore or suppress your feelings. Instead, you create space to acknowledge them without letting them control your behavior.

4. Increases Resilience

Regular mindfulness practice makes you more resilient to stress over time. You will notice that the things that used to rattle you don't have the same effect anymore. You can approach challenges with clarity and a calmer mind.

My Shivers

Let me take you back to a time when I found myself in a situation so uncommon that it felt like I was living in a scene from a movie.

It was a winter afternoon, and I was sitting in my office, prepping for a big meeting the next day. The room was quiet, save for distant sound of traffic outside. I worked tirelessly for weeks, pouring my heart and soul into this project for a high-stakes client looking to revolutionize the hospitality industry.

Now, I am a planner by nature. I thrive on organization and order, so when my boss casually mentioned a last-minute addition to the project plan – an unexpected live demo – I felt the ground beneath me shift.

A live demo of project components? With only a day to prepare? My mind instantly spiraled into chaos, picturing everything that could go wrong – technical glitches, an uninterested audience, or worse – failing to impress our client.

As I sat there, my anxiety manifested physically. My palms were sweaty, and I could feel my heart pounding like a bass drum. In sheer panic, I dashed to the break room for a quick cup of coffee. But standing there, watching the coffee drip into my cup, I realized I had hit a wall. I was in a fight-or-flight mode, fueled by stress, and it was paralyzing.

Suddenly, the fire alarm went off. Loud, blaring, and completely unexpected. As my colleagues began to shuffle toward the exit, I felt the world's weight on my shoulders. I was already overwhelmed, and now there was a real emergency. We poured out of the building, the cold air hitting me like a slap.

Outside, we gathered in a safe zone while the Emergency Response Team checked the building. I stood there, feeling trapped between the urgency of the situation and the looming anxiety of the project plan presentation. My colleagues were chatting nervously, some cracking jokes, others checking their phones for updates. I felt detached, like an observer in a surreal dream.

As I paced back and forth, my thoughts raced. I had already lost precious time I could have used to prepare for the demo, and I still had no clear idea of how to execute it. At that moment, I remembered I had read about mindfulness – taking a moment to breathe and be present.

I stepped aside from the crowd and found a quiet spot under a large mango tree. I took a deep breath, inhaling the earthy scent of fallen leaves, grounding myself in the moment. As I exhaled, I closed my eyes. I focused on the sounds around me – the rustling of leaves, the distant chatter of my colleagues, even the faint sirens of emergency vehicles.

Instead of thinking about the presentation of project plan, I allowed myself to acknowledge my feelings – anxiety, pressure, frustration – and then let them go. I visualized my worries as leaves floating down a stream, gently carried away by the current. This wasn't easy initially. My mind kept racing back to the project plan, but I persisted. Slowly, I felt my body begin to relax. The tightness in my chest eased, and I realized that, at this moment, everything was okay.

After about ten minutes, I opened my eyes and returned to the group, feeling lighter and more focused. I felt a new sense of clarity as we were allowed back into the building. I wasn't entirely sure how I would pull off the project plan. Still, I knew I could approach it without the suffocating weight of anxiety dragging me down.

When I returned to my desk, I took a moment to outline a new project plan. Instead of obsessing over every detail of the presentation, I focused on the key milestones I wanted to convey. I also incorporated a short explanation of one part of the project rather than relying solely on a entire detail. It allowed me to illustrate the salient points while minimizing potential technicalities.

The next day, I walked into the meeting room with a newfound sense of confidence. I introduced the short explanation of the project and then explained the project milestones as part of project plan. The atmosphere in the room shifted. My colleagues were engaged nodding, and the client seemed genuinely impressed. When the presentation finished, I was met with enthusiastic appreciation.

While stress is an inevitable part of life, how we respond to it makes all the difference. The fire alarm that day wasn't just a disruption, it became an opportunity for me to practice mindfulness unexpectedly.

I realized that mindfulness doesn't always have to be a formal practice or something reserved for quiet moments of meditation. Sometimes, it's about finding those moments of clarity amidst the chaos. I transformed an overwhelming situation into a manageable one by taking just a few minutes to center myself.

I committed to incorporating mindfulness into my work routine from that day forward. Whether through brief breathing exercises before meetings or mindful breaks when stress began to creep in, I found that my ability to handle pressure improved dramatically. I became more resilient, and my productivity soared.

That unexpected fire drill taught me more than just how to manage a presentation. It highlighted the power of mindfulness as a tool for navigating the unpredictable nature of our work lives. Stress may be a constant presence, but with mindfulness, we can learn to navigate it with grace and clarity.

How You Can Start Using Mindfulness at Work

If you are thinking, *'That sounds great, but where do I start?'* don't worry. Mindfulness doesn't need to be complicated or time-consuming.

Here are a few simple ways to start integrating mindfulness into your workday:

1. Mindful breathing

Focus on your breath for a few moments throughout the day. You don't have to stop what you are doing –bring your awareness to the sensation of your breath entering and leaving your body. This can be particularly helpful during stressful moments or before a big meeting.

2. Body scan

When feeling tense, do a quick body scan. Close your eyes (if possible) and notice where you are holding tension. Maybe it's in your shoulders, your jaw, or your back. Take a deep breath and consciously release the tension in that area.

3. Single-tasking

Rather than juggling multiple tasks at once, focus on one task at a time. Give it your full attention. When your mind starts to wander (and it will), gently bring it back to the task.

4. Mindful listening

In meetings or conversations, practice truly listening without planning your response or getting distracted by other thoughts. Focus entirely on the person speaking, their words, and the tone of their voice. You will be amazed at how much more you retain and how much more connected you will feel to your colleagues.

5. Take mindful breaks

Instead of scrolling through your phone during breaks, try stepping outside or sitting quietly for a few minutes. Pay attention to the sensations around you–the sun's warmth, the sounds of nature, or even the hum of office life. This short mental reset can do wonders for your Focus and energy.

The Long-Term Impact of Mindfulness on Stress

Mindfulness isn't a magic cure for workplace stress but a powerful tool for managing it. Over time, with consistent practice, mindfulness can help you develop a new relationship with stress. Instead of being consumed by it, you learn to observe, understand, and ultimately reduce its impact on your well-being.

Taking care of your mental and emotional health is supremely essential. Incorporating mindfulness into your daily routine will make you more resilient to stress and enhance your overall work performance and satisfaction.

Remember, stress is inevitable, but suffering because of it is optional. Mindfulness is your way to navigate through the storm with clarity and calmness.

'Between stimulus and response, there is a space. In that space is our power to choose our response. In our response lies our growth and our freedom.' – Victor Frankl

17.

Fostering Creativity and Innovation

In moments rushed, the mind will race,
But stillness finds its quiet place.
A breath, a pause, to slow the pace,
And stress begins to lose its trace.
In mindful calm, we learn to see,
The peace within sets us free.

'Creativity is thinking up new things. Innovation is doing new things.' – Theodore Levitt

Creativity and Innovation are always overlooked in our work lives.

Beyond buzzwords, they are essential ingredients for any organization aiming to thrive. However, fostering creativity and innovation can feel like trying to catch smoke with your bare hands.

So why is this the case? Why is promoting creativity and innovation such a common hurdle in workplaces, and how can we overcome it together?

Understanding the Creativity Conundrum

Many workplaces paradoxically stifle creativity in a world that demands fresh ideas and innovative solutions. Rigid hierarchies, strict processes, and a pervasive fear of failure often create an environment where employees feel hesitant to share their thoughts or explore unconventional ideas. You know exactly what I mean if you have ever sat through a meeting where the same ideas were regurgitated.

I remember being part of a team for a large-sized tech company. We had just launched a new project and knew we needed to innovate to shorten timelines to finish the project. But every time we tried to brainstorm new ideas, the same voices dominated the conversation.

Fear loomed over the room, silencing the more creative, outside-the-box thinkers. I quickly realized that our reluctance to explore new possibilities prevented us from tapping into the full potential of our team.

Why Creativity Matters

Before we dive into strategies for fostering creativity and innovation, let's take a moment to understand why they matter.

1. **Adapting to Change**

The businesses are constantly evolving. Companies that foster creativity are more adaptable and can pivot quickly when market trends shift. This adaptability is crucial for long-term survival.

2. **Improving Problem-Solving**

Creative teams are better at problem-solving. When faced with challenges, they are more likely to develop innovative solutions instead of resorting to the same old methods.

3. **Enhancing Employee Engagement**

Employees who feel empowered to share their ideas are more engaged and invested in their work. This leads to higher job satisfaction and retention rates.

4. **Gaining Competitive Advantage**

Companies prioritizing innovation often stand out in their industries. They are more likely to capture customers' attention and outperform their competitors.

Breaking Down Barriers to Creativity

So, how do we break down the barriers that stifle creativity and innovation? Here are several strategies to consider:

1. Create a Safe Space for Ideas

First and foremost, creating a safe environment where team members feel comfortable sharing their ideas is essential. This means fostering a culture that values diverse perspectives and encourages risk-taking.

As leaders, we must remind our teams that not every idea has to be a winner, *'bad'* ideas can often lead to the best ones.

Creating a non-judgmental atmosphere is crucial. You might think, *'This is just common sense!'* but you would be surprised how many workplaces fail to implement this simple yet vital principle.

In my team, we instituted a practice called *'Idea Hour.'* Every fortnight, we set aside time for brainstorming without any judgment. The only rule? There are no bad ideas. This shift in approach opened the floodgates for creativity.

For instance, one day, someone pitched creating an interactive online quiz about our project – something we hadn't considered before. This idea eventually became one of the best practices, driving engagement and interest in our project.

2. Encourage Collaboration

Next, encourage Collaboration across different departments. Sometimes, the best ideas come from unexpected places. By breaking down silos and facilitating cross-functional teams, you can spark innovation in ways you might never have anticipated.

Bringing together diverse teams can lead to breakthroughs. For example, when we faced a challenge with product positioning, we invited members from sales, customer service, and even IT to our brainstorming session. This mix of perspectives led to insights that were critical in reshaping our approach and connecting with our audience more meaningfully.

Imagine how different departments can contribute unique insights – the sales team understands customer pain points. At the same time, IT can provide insights into the technical feasibility of new ideas. Tapping into this collective intelligence can be a game-changer.

3. Celebrate Experimentation and Learn from Failure

Not every idea will be a success, and that's perfectly okay. In fact, failure can be one of our best teachers. When we celebrate experimentation and frame failures as learning opportunities, we encourage our teams to take calculated risks without the fear of repercussions.

In our *'Idea Hour,'* we dedicated some time to reflecting on past projects that didn't go as planned. Instead of viewing these as failures, we discussed what we learned from each experience. This reflection not only reinforced the idea that failure is part of the process but also helped us refine our future strategies.

Cultivating an Innovative Mindset

Fostering a culture of creativity and innovation is about more than just implementing new practices, it's about cultivating a mindset that embraces change and encourages Curiosity. Here are some practical steps to help nurture this mindset within your organization –

1. Encourage Curiosity

Curiosity is the foundation of creativity. Encourage your team to ask questions and explore new ideas. Consider implementing regular *'Curiosity Challenges,'* where team members research a topic outside their expertise and present their findings. This not only broadens their horizons but can also inspire new ideas related to your work.

2. Provide Resources for Growth

Investing in your team's development is essential for fostering creativity. Consider providing access to workshops, online courses, or industry conferences. The more knowledge and skills your team members acquire, the more innovative ideas they can bring to the table.

I remember attending a marketing conference where I learned about cutting-edge trends in digital marketing.

When I returned, I was bursting with ideas that ultimately shaped our marketing strategy for the better.

3. Establish Clear Goals

Having clear goals can help guide your team's creative efforts. Set innovation-related objectives that align with your organization's overall strategy. This provides a framework for brainstorming sessions and encourages team members to think creatively within those parameters.

Real-Life Impact: A Journey to Innovation

Going back to my earlier experience, after implementing these strategies, we saw a remarkable shift. Not only did our creativity flourish, but we also experienced an increase in employee engagement and satisfaction.

When team members felt that their voices mattered and that their ideas could lead to real change, they became more invested in their work. The interactive quiz we created became a viral hit and significantly boosted our product's visibility.

But the impact didn't stop there. We noticed a change in our team's atmosphere. Meetings became livelier, Collaboration increased, and new ideas flowed freely. This transformation reaffirmed my belief in the power of fostering creativity and innovation.

Overcoming Resistance to Change

Now, you might be thinking, *'This sounds great, but my team is resistant to change.'* That's a valid concern. Change can be daunting, especially if your team is used to a particular way of doing things. Here are some strategies to help overcome that resistance:

1. Involve Employees in the process

Involving employees in the decision-making process can significantly reduce resistance. When team members feel that their opinions matter, they are more likely to buy into new initiatives. Consider conducting surveys or hosting focus groups to gather input on proposed changes.

2. Communicate the Benefits

Clearly articulate the benefits of fostering creativity and innovation. Share success stories from your organization or industry to demonstrate the positive impact of these efforts. When team members see tangible results, they will be more inclined to embrace change.

3. Start Small

If your organization is resistant to change, start small. Implement one or two strategies for fostering creativity and innovation, and then gradually build on those successes. This approach allows your team to adapt to new practices without feeling overwhelmed.

Measuring the Impact of Creativity and Innovation

To truly understand the effectiveness of your efforts, it's essential to measure the impact of fostering creativity and innovation within your organization. Here are some key metrics to consider:

1. Employee Engagement Surveys

Conduct regular employee engagement surveys to gauge how your team feels about their ability to contribute ideas and collaborate. Look for trends over time to see if your initiatives are making a difference.

2. Innovation Metrics

Track the number of new ideas generated, implemented, and the resulting impact on your business. This could include metrics such as sales growth from new products, customer satisfaction scores, or improvements in efficiency.

3. Feedback Loops

Create feedback loops where employees can share their thoughts on the effectiveness of your initiatives. This can help you refine your approach and ensure that you are meeting the needs of your team.

The Road Ahead

Fostering creativity and innovation is not just a one-time initiative. It's an ongoing journey. By creating a culture that embraces diverse ideas, encourages Collaboration, and learns from failure, we can unlock the full potential of our teams.

So, what's stopping you from starting this journey in your own workplace? Remember, it takes time, patience, and a commitment to change. But the rewards? There are absolutely worth it. Let's create workplaces where innovation thrives, ideas flow freely, and creativity is celebrated. Together, we can transform our work environments into hubs of inspiration and ingenuity.

Final Thoughts

In closing, I encourage you to take a moment and reflect on your workplace culture. Are you fostering an environment that nurtures creativity and innovation? If not, it's never too late to start. Embrace the challenge, get your team involved, and embark on this journey together.

Let's break free from the chains of conventional thinking and create a vibrant culture of creativity. Your organization and your employees will thank you for it.

'Innovation distinguishes between a leader and a follower.' – Steve Jobs

18.

Adapting to Change and Uncertainty

In the face of change, we often fear,
The unknown paths that aren't yet clear.
But storms of doubt can shape our way,
And guide us toward a brighter day.
For those who bend, but do not break,
Will find new strength in each leap they take.

'The measure of intelligence is the ability to change.' – Albert Einstein

Imagine this, you walk into the office on a seemingly ordinary Monday morning, coffee in hand, ready to tackle the day's tasks. But within minutes, you are blindsided. An email hits your inbox with the subject line: *'Urgent Team Restructure – Immediate Effect.'* The company's leadership has announced a massive shakeup. Your team is changing, your role might be in jeopardy, and suddenly, everything feels like it's spiraling out of control.

Your heart races. Anxiety creeps in. Questions swirl in your mind: What does this mean for me? Will I have to learn new skills? Will I even have a job next month?

Sound familiar?

Change and uncertainty in the workplace have a way of hitting us like a freight train – unexpected, disorienting, and often leaving us scrambling to regain our footing. But what if I told you that these moments, as unsettling as they are, hold the potential for your most extraordinary growth? What if navigating uncertainty could unlock new opportunities you never saw coming?

Let's dive into the chaos and discover how to not just survive change but thrive in it.

The Nature of Change and Uncertainty

First, let's acknowledge one thing, change is hard. Uncertainty is uncomfortable. As human beings, we tend to find comfort in stability, routine, and predictability. It's part of our wiring. We feel safer when we know what is coming next. In a workplace setting, it's tempting to settle into familiar patterns, processes, and relationships. But as much as we crave that security, change is inevitable. You can count on it.

In a professional environment, change can come in many forms:

- **Technological advancements:** Suddenly, you are required to learn a whole new software system or technology that makes your old processes obsolete.
- **Organizational shifts:** A restructure happens, and you are now reporting to a different boss or your role changes.
- **Economic fluctuations:** The market dips, budgets shrink, or the demand for your company's product drops.
- **Team dynamics:** Key team members leave, or new hires bring a different energy and dynamic to the group.
- **Pandemics and global events:** Need I say more? The pandemic upended everything, from where we work to how we communicate with each other.

Uncertainty often follows these changes. Will you be able to keep up with the new tools? How will your relationship with your new boss affect your growth? What if the budget cuts mean layoffs? The ambiguity can feel overwhelming, even paralyzing.

But here is the thing – while we can't always control the changes that happen, we can control how we respond to them. And that's what adapting to change and uncertainty is all about.

Why Adaptability is Key in the Workplace

Imagine a company that refuses to change. Maybe they refuse to adopt new technologies, or they don't address changes in consumer behavior. Eventually, that company is going to get left behind. The same principle applies to individuals. If you are not willing or able to adjust to the changing conditions of your job, your team, or your industry, you risk becoming obsolete.

Adaptability is a critical skill in today's job market. In fact, more and more employers are looking for people who are flexible, open to new ideas, and able to learn quickly. However, adaptability is not just about being able to change direction when needed. It's about maintaining a positive mindset during periods of uncertainty, being willing to step outside your comfort zone, and even finding opportunities in the chaos.

A Real-Life Example of Change and Uncertainty

A few years back, I was working for a company that was growing quickly. Things were going well, and the team was energized. However, out of the blue, the company underwent a massive restructuring. My team was reshuffled, and suddenly, I found myself reporting to a new manager who had a completely different style and set of expectations.

At first, it was disorienting. I had built a strong rapport with my previous boss, and now I was back at square one. The uncertainty didn't stop there. Rumors about layoffs and budget cuts were circulating. The entire office was on edge, wondering what would happen next. No one knew if the projects we were working on would be funded or if we would even have jobs in a few months.

I remember feeling a mix of anxiety and frustration. For weeks, I operated in survival mode, just waiting for the other shoe to drop. But here is where the shift happened, I realized that I couldn't change what was happening around me, but I could change how I was responding to it.

I decided to have an open conversation with my new manager to understand her expectations and style. I proactively sought out ways to align myself with the new goals of the team. Instead of waiting for direction, I started suggesting new ideas and offering to take on projects that would help us transition through the changes.

Was it easy? No. But by embracing the uncertainty, I became more resilient. I learned how to communicate more effectively, build new relationships, and, most importantly, maintain my sanity during the turbulence. That experience not only helped me grow professionally but also taught me valuable life lessons about adaptability and resilience.

The Emotional Side of Change and Uncertainty

Let's talk about the emotional side of dealing with change because it's real and can be challenging. It's okay to admit that when the rug gets pulled out from under you, it stings.

When we are hit with an unexpected change or we are left in a cloud of uncertainty, it's normal to experience emotions like anxiety, frustration, or even anger.

In the workplace, these emotions can affect your performance and overall well-being. Maybe you are feeling less motivated because you are unsure if your work will even matter in a few months. Or perhaps the changes make you question your future with the company. These emotional reactions are human, but it's important not to let them take control.

Here are a few ways to manage the emotional turbulence that comes with change –

1. Acknowledge your feelings

It's okay to feel uneasy or anxious about changes. Pretending everything is fine when it's not will only bottle up your emotions, leading to burnout.

2. Talk about it

Find someone to talk to – whether it's a colleague, friend, or mentor. Sometimes, just expressing how you are feeling can lift a massive weight off your shoulders.

3. Focus on what you can control

There is a lot you can't control during times of uncertainty, but what you can control is how you approach the situation. Are you being proactive? Are you taking steps to understand the changes instead of resisting them?

4. Practice self-care

When the workplace feels chaotic, it's even more important to take care of yourself. Whether it's exercise, meditation, or simply taking a break, making time for self-care will keep your mind and body ready to face challenges.

Strategies for Adapting to Change and Uncertainty

Alright, we have talked about the nature of change, why adaptability is essential, and how to manage your emotions. Now, let's get practical. Here are some strategies you can use to adapt to change and uncertainty in the workplace:

1. Stay Open-Minded

When changes happen, it's easy to go into defense mode and resist. But resisting change only makes it more challenging. Instead, try to adopt an open-minded attitude. Ask yourself, *'What can I learn from this?'* or *'How can this benefit me or my team?'* Viewing change as an opportunity instead of a threat can drastically shift your perspective.

2. Focus on Skill Development

In times of uncertainty, one of the best things you can do is invest in yourself. Whether it's learning new technical skills, improving your communication abilities, or gaining a better understanding of your industry, continuous learning will keep you adaptable. Plus, developing new skills will make you more valuable, regardless of what changes come your way.

3. Be Proactive

Don't wait for things to settle before taking action. If you sense that changes are coming, be proactive. Seek out information, ask questions, and clarify expectations with your manager or team. Taking initiative during periods of uncertainty shows leadership and makes you a valuable team member.

4. Build a Support Network

One of the most challenging aspects of dealing with change is feeling like you are in it alone. Cultivate a network of colleagues, mentors, and friends who can offer guidance, feedback, or just a listening ear. Not only will this help you gain perspective, but it will also provide emotional support when things get tough.

5. Embrace Flexibility

Flexibility is crucial in navigating change. This might mean being willing to take on new roles, shift your responsibilities, or even rethink how you approach your work. The more adaptable you are, the more opportunities you will find, even in the midst of uncertainty.

6. Maintain a Positive Attitude

I am not talking about toxic positivity – where you try to ignore problems by pretending everything is perfect. However, having a generally positive mindset helps you see challenges as opportunities rather than roadblocks.

When others are panicking or feeling overwhelmed, maintaining an optimistic outlook can help you stand out and keep your focus on solutions.

7. Reflect on Past Experiences

Think back to times when you have faced uncertainty or had to navigate change in the past. How did you handle it? What did you learn from those experiences? Often, reminding yourself that you have successfully dealt with change before can boost your confidence when facing new challenges.

Wrapping Up

In the end, adapting to change and uncertainty in the workplace is a skill that takes practice. It's not about pretending change is easy or that uncertainty is fun – it's about developing the mindset and strategies to face those challenges with resilience and optimism.

It's likely that at some point, you will face a situation similar to mine – where everything feels up in the air, and you are unsure of what's coming next. But instead of letting fear or frustration take over, try to lean into the uncertainty. Be proactive, be flexible, and remember that change, while uncomfortable, often leads to growth.

'It is not the strongest of the species that survive, nor the most intelligent, but the one most responsive to change.' – Charles Darwin

19.

Building Trust and Accountability

In a world where roles entwine,
Trust is the bridge that we design.
With open hearts, our voices blend,
In every challenge, we must defend.
Together we rise, in unity we stand,
Building a future, hand in hand.

'Accountability breeds response-ability.' – Stephen R. Covey

A simple truth – Trust and Accountability are the cornerstones of any successful workplace.

You can have the most skilled team in the world. Still, if trust is lacking, everything suffers – collaboration, morale, and ultimately, performance. Without accountability, tasks fall through the cracks, deadlines are missed, and resentment can build among team members.

But here's the tricky part: building trust and fostering accountability is often a hurdle that many workplaces face. It's not that people don't want to trust one another or take responsibility for their work – it's just that creating the right environment for these values to thrive is much harder than it seems. Trust has to be earned, accountability has to be encouraged, and both need to be reinforced consistently.

You might be asking yourself, *'How do I foster trust and accountability in my team? What can I do to build a more connected, responsible work culture?'* In this chapter, we will dive into why these values are so important and how you can actively cultivate them in your workplace.

Understanding Trust: Why It's So Hard to Build and So Easy to Lose

Think of trust like a bank account. You make small deposits over time through honest communication, follow-through, and reliability. But one broken promise? One instance of miscommunication? It's like withdrawing all those deposits in one go. Rebuilding it is possible, but it takes time and effort.

In a work environment, trust looks like this – employees believe that their leaders have their best interests in mind, colleagues trust that they can rely on each other to do what they say they will do, and everyone feels comfortable enough to share ideas, give feedback, or ask for help.

The issue is trust can feel fragile, and small moments of mistrust can erode it quickly. I have seen this happen firsthand in my own career. I remember a time when I was working on a big project with a team where trust was shaky. Deadlines were approaching fast, and there was little room for error. One of my teammates, let's call him Gopal, had promised to complete a crucial part of the project. We had an understanding that he would communicate any delays or issues early on so we could pivot if necessary.

However, as the deadline loomed closer, Gopal wasn't as communicative as we needed. We assumed everything was on track, only to find out – right before the deadline – that he had hit some major roadblocks and the work was far from finished.

Not only did we have to scramble to pick up the pieces, but the trust we had in Gopal took a hit. The worst part wasn't that the task was incomplete (everyone hits roadblocks at times) but that he didn't communicate the problem when he first encountered it. From then on, every time Gopal said, *'I have got it under control,'* we couldn't help but wonder if he really did. That lack of trust made collaboration more difficult and stressful for everyone involved.

Takeaway here – In any workplace, when people don't feel like they can rely on their colleagues to be transparent or dependable, they start to micromanage, second-guess, and disengage. And that's a recipe for dysfunction.

So, How Do We Build Trust?

1. Consistency is Key

Trust is built on predictability. If you say you are going to do something, do it. If something comes up and you can't communicate it as soon as possible, even in Gopal's case, if he had just been upfront about his challenges, our trust wouldn't have been broken. People understand that roadblocks happen, but they can't work with what they don't know.

2. Open Communication

Encourage an environment where it's okay to ask questions, express concerns, or give feedback. The more openly people can communicate, the fewer misunderstandings will arise. Regular check-ins, team meetings, or even casual one-on-ones can create the space for transparent conversations.

3. Be Vulnerable

Trust isn't about perfection. In fact, admitting when you don't have all the answers or when you have made a mistake can increase trust. It shows humility and openness. Leaders who are vulnerable set the tone for their teams, making it easier for others to do the same.

4. Follow Through on Commitments

Accountability and trust go hand in hand. When people see that you consistently keep your word, they trust you more. If something is beyond your control, be upfront about it, but always try to find a solution or alternative.

Accountability: The Other Side of the Coin

While trust is about relationships, accountability is about responsibility. It's the glue that holds everything together when you are working in a team. Without it, things fall apart. Accountability means that every person owns their role, their responsibilities, and the outcomes – good or bad.

We often think about accountability in terms of reprimanding someone when things go wrong, but it's not just about holding people to task when mistakes happen. Real accountability starts with clear expectations and support. It's about setting people up for success and ensuring they understand what's expected of them.

Accountability Gone Wrong

Let's dive deeper into that situation where accountability slipped through the cracks, leading to a major project derailment. I want to set the stage for you to truly grasp the impact of what happened.

The Background

Our team was buzzing with excitement. We had been awarded a contract for a new construction project that promised to be a significant addition to our Client. This

Client center would serve as a hub for activities and events. Everyone was invested – the architects were finalizing the design, the construction crew was eager to break ground, and the operations team was preparing for a smooth workflow.

As the project manager, Sunil was responsible for coordinating all these moving parts. The launch date was set, and everyone was looking forward to seeing our hard work come to life. However, as we dove deeper into the project, the atmosphere shifted. Tension was mounting, and I could sense that something was off.

The Breakdown: Who's in Charge?

As Sunil split the project into different components, we assigned various roles and responsibilities to team members. The architects were responsible for the design, the construction crew was tasked with building, and the operations team was set to ensure that everything was in place for inspections and permits. However, Sunil failed to define who was ultimately responsible for overseeing the project as a whole.

Each team assumed that someone else was managing the overall timeline and deliverables. The construction crew was focused on on-site building, the architects were busy with the design details, and the operations team was preparing for the necessary inspections and approvals. However, none took a step back to ensure everything was aligning as planned. It was a classic case of *'Who's got this?'* And unfortunately, the answer was nobody.

The Consequence: A Missed Completion Deadline

As the critical midpoint of the project approached, Sunil began to notice warning signs. Deadlines were slipping, and updates were becoming increasingly sparse. He assumed that each team was keeping an eye on their responsibilities, but when he finally called a meeting to check in on progress, he was met with blank stares and a collective realization that we were in trouble.

The construction crew had encountered unexpected issues with the site's soil quality that had delayed their timeline, but they had assumed someone would inform the operations team about these delays so that inspections could be rescheduled. The operations team, on the other hand, had been finalizing their plans for a timely completion without knowing that the construction was falling behind.

When Sunil finally put all the pieces together, it was too late. He had to postpone the handover, which meant delaying the project's completion and affecting his relationship with the Client. The impact rippled through the entire organization, resulting in lost opportunities and a dented reputation.

The Aftermath: Frustration and Learning

After the dust settled, Sunil gathered the team to discuss what had gone wrong. The atmosphere was tense, and there was an air of frustration. Everyone was pointing fingers, and he realized that blame wasn't going to help him move forward. It was clear that he had made assumptions about accountability that led him to this point.

In the end, he identified the root causes of his failure. The lack of clear ownership and the absence of regular check-ins contributed significantly to his downfall. He learned that accountability doesn't just mean completing tasks. It also means ensuring that everyone is aligned and aware of the bigger picture.

To prevent this from happening again, he established a new protocol for future projects. He created a detailed project charter that outlined each team member's roles and responsibilities, set clear deadlines, and included checkpoints for progress updates. He also instituted regular cross-team meetings to foster communication and ensure that everyone was on the same page.

A Valuable Lesson

This experience taught him a powerful lesson about the importance of accountability in a collaborative environment. Accountability isn't just about holding people responsible for their tasks. It's about creating a culture where everyone understands how their work fits into the larger mission and feels empowered to communicate challenges as they arise.

Looking back, Sunil saw that the missing link was their collective understanding of accountability. Had he clarified who was responsible for overseeing the project and established a process for regular communication, he could have avoided the last-minute scramble and ensured a successful launch.

Ultimately, this experience transformed the approach to teamwork. Sunil became more intentional about fostering a culture of accountability, which in turn led to greater trust among his team members. By learning from his mistakes and focusing on clear roles, open communication, and collective ownership, he built a stronger foundation for future projects. This not only improved their performances but also deepened relationships, setting the stage for a more collaborative and successful work environment.

Accountability isn't just about checking boxes. It was about making sure everyone felt responsible for the shared success of the team. And that's a lesson from Sunil's situation I carry with me to this day.

How to Create Accountability in Your Workplace

1. Set Clear Expectations

This seems obvious, but it's surprising how often teams jump into tasks without fully understanding what success looks like. Make sure that everyone knows precisely what is expected of them and, more importantly, why their role matters to the overall goal.

2. Assign Roles and Ownership

One of the biggest mistakes in accountability is assuming someone else is handling something. Avoid this by clearly assigning ownership of tasks or projects. When everyone knows who is responsible for what, there's less confusion and more forward momentum.

3. Foster a Culture of Feedback

Accountability isn't just about waiting for things to go wrong. Regular feedback – both positive and constructive – is critical. When people feel supported and guided, they are more likely to take responsibility for their actions and outcomes.

4. Celebrate Wins and Learn from Mistakes

Accountability also means recognizing when things go well and acknowledging those responsible. Celebrate wins as a team, and when things don't go as planned, use those moments as learning opportunities rather than finger-pointing sessions.

The Intersection of Trust and Accountability

Trust and accountability feed into each other. When people feel like they can trust their colleagues, they are more willing to take responsibility for their work. Likewise, when people are held accountable in a supportive way, it fosters an environment where trust can thrive.

For example, in teams where trust is high, individuals aren't afraid to admit when there are struggling with a task because they know their teammates will offer support instead of judgment. On the flip side, in environments where accountability is strong, trust grows because people consistently follow through on their commitments.

Let me take you back to the story with Gopal. After the project fiasco, our team had a serious conversation – not just with Gopal but with each other. We agreed to be more upfront about potential problems and to communicate any obstacles early on. Gopal admitted that he didn't speak up because he didn't want to let the team down, but in doing so, Gopal realized he had let us down even more by not being honest. From that point on, we made accountability a priority, and the trust between us began to rebuild. The experience taught us that both trust and accountability are necessary for any team to function well.

Practical Tips to Implement Today

Here are a few actionable steps to help you build trust and accountability in your workplace:

1. **Set the Tone as a Leader**

   Whether you are a manager or a team member, model the behavior you want to see. Be reliable, communicate openly, and take responsibility for your actions. Your example will set the standard for others.

2. **Create Accountability Structures**

   Use tools like project management software or accountability partners to ensure that everyone's roles and responsibilities are clear. Having these systems in place helps prevent things from slipping through the cracks.

3. **Hold Regular Check-ins**

A simple way to build trust and ensure accountability is through regular, structured check-ins. These can be one-on-one meetings, team catch-ups, or progress reviews where everyone has the opportunity to discuss challenges, ask for help, or share updates.

4. **Acknowledge Both Effort and Outcome**

It's important to recognize when people are trying their best, even if things don't go perfectly. This creates a culture where people feel safe to take risks, which in turn builds trust. At the same time, acknowledge when people deliver on their promises, reinforcing the importance of accountability.

Trust and Accountability – A Continuous Effort

Building trust and accountability isn't a one-and-done task. It's an ongoing process that requires effort, communication, and a commitment to growth. The reality is that even in the best teams, trust can be shaken, and accountability can slip. But create a culture where these values are prioritized. You will be able to overcome challenges, foster collaboration, and set your team up for success.

At the end of the day, trust and accountability aren't just workplace buzzwords – they are the building blocks of any thriving, high-performing team. By consistently focusing on these values, you will create an environment where people feel supported, empowered, and ready to do their best work.

'Trust is the glue of life. It's the most essential ingredient in effective communication. It's the foundational principle that holds all relationships.'
– Stephen R. Covey

20.

Celebrating Success – Recognition and Appreciation

In the quiet hum of dreams pursued,
We gather strength, our hopes renewed.
Through trials faced and victories won,
Let laughter ring, our hearts as one.
For in the joy of shared delight,
We find our purpose, our spirits ignite.

'Success is best when it's shared.' – Howard Schultz

Picture this – a dimly lit conference room, the air thick with anticipation, and the flickering glow of laptops illuminating the tired faces of a team that has poured their heart and soul into their work. The clock ticks ominously towards the deadline, a relentless reminder of the mounting pressure. Just outside, the world buzzes with excitement, but inside, the atmosphere is electric with anxiety.

After weeks of work, endless revisions, and countless cups of coffee, they are on the brink of a breakthrough. In just moments, they will present a proposal that could make or break their reputation – a chance to rise from the shadows and bask in the glory of success or falter under the weight of expectation.

As they gather around the table, they share not just their hopes but their fears. Will their efforts be fruitful? Will they be celebrated, or will they slip quietly into the background, their triumph forgotten? This is not just a project. It's a defining moment, a chance to prove their worth and validate the countless hours they have sacrificed.

Little do they know, the true victory lies not just in the success that awaits them but in the celebration of their journey – a lesson that would reshape their understanding of achievement and the power of acknowledgment in a world too often fixated on the next challenge.

The Importance of Celebrating Success

Basics first, why is celebrating success so important?

Well, for one, it boosts morale. When we acknowledge our accomplishments – big or small – we create a positive work environment around. Think about it, when was the last time you felt truly appreciated for your efforts? Those moments of recognition can energize us, fostering a sense of belonging and teamwork.

Celebrating success also reinforces desired behaviors and encourages future achievements. Suppose an employee or team feels recognized for their hard work. In that case, they are more likely to replicate those behaviors in the future.

In contrast, when success goes unnoticed, motivation can wane, leading to disengagement. This is particularly true where people are often caught up in the grind of daily tasks.

Overcoming the Hurdles

Now, let's discuss some common hurdles that prevent us from celebrating success in the workplace.

1. The *'Keep Moving'* Culture

One of the primary reasons we struggle with celebrating success is the pervasive *'keep moving'* culture. In many workplaces, there's a relentless push to stay productive and keep the momentum going. While it's great to strive for progress, it can create an environment where achievements are overlooked. Instead of taking a moment to appreciate our wins, we quickly move on to the next project.

2. Fear of Complacency

There is also a fear that celebrating success might lead to complacency. Some leaders worry that if their teams get too comfortable with recognition, they will stop pushing for excellence. However, this line of thinking can be detrimental. Celebrating success doesn't mean we stop striving for improvement. Instead, it helps us maintain a healthy balance between recognizing our achievements and setting new goals.

3. Lack of Structure

Many organizations lack a structured approach to recognition and celebration. While informal shout-outs can be effective, having a formal recognition program can ensure that success is consistently celebrated across the board. Without a plan, celebrations may feel random or sporadic, which can diminish their impact.

Creating a Culture of Celebration

So, how do we create a culture of celebration in our workplaces? Here are a few strategies:

1. Set Clear Goals and Metrics

First, it's essential to establish clear goals and metrics for success. When everyone knows what there are working towards, it becomes easier to recognize when those goals are achieved. Whether it's hitting a sales target, completing a project on time, or receiving positive client feedback, having specific benchmarks helps clarify what success looks like.

2. Encourage Peer Recognition

Encouraging peer recognition can be incredibly powerful. Create opportunities for team members to acknowledge each other's contributions. This could be through a dedicated channel on your team's communication platform or a monthly meeting where employees can share shout-outs. When we recognize each other, it builds camaraderie and strengthens team dynamics.

3. Celebrate Often, But Meaningfully

Celebrations don't always have to be grand events. Small, meaningful acknowledgments can be just as impactful. Whether it's a heartfelt email, a shout-out during a team meeting, or a fun team lunch, taking the time to celebrate can make a world of difference.

The Team That Turned Challenges into Triumph

Let me take you back a few years to my time at a mid-sized organization. We were a tight-knit group of professionals working on a high-stakes project for a major client. The pressure was immense, and the stakes were even higher. If we succeed, it could mean a substantial boost to our reputation and future opportunities. If we failed, the consequences would be significant.

The Challenge

The project was a chateau type of 100 dwelling units – novel, elegant, and opulent. Our client had high expectations and a strict deadline, giving us only 24 months to execute the entire project. The moment we received the contract, a wave of excitement washed over the organization, but that excitement quickly morphed into anxiety as the reality of our task set in.

As the months rolled on, we faced an uphill battle. The client was constantly shifting their vision, throwing us curveballs that made it challenging to stay focused. It felt like we were chasing a moving target, and every time we thought we had a solid direction, something changed. Late nights became the norm, and team morale began to dip. I could see the strain on my colleagues' faces, and I felt it, too.

The Breakthrough Moment

Then, one Friday afternoon, after another long week of brainstorming, we decided that we needed a break. I called for an impromptu *'Fun Friday'* meeting – something lighthearted to lift spirits. (Some organisation celebrate TGIF)

We gathered in our cozy office on site, and instead of diving into the usual project-related talk, I brought out a board game. At first, there were groans. Some team members were too tired to play. But I insisted, believing we needed this moment of levity.

To my surprise, the laughter that erupted during that game transformed the atmosphere. The stress seemed to melt away as we shared silly jokes and friendly competition. In those moments, we were reminded of our bond – not just as colleagues but as friends.

As the game wrapped up, something shifted. Inspired by our lightheartedness, one of my teammates, Jeevan, shared a breakthrough idea for the project that had come to him during our game. It was fresh, innovative, and unlike anything we had done before. We all rallied around it, energized by the renewed camaraderie and the collective joy we had just experienced. That single idea became the cornerstone of our project progress.

The Final Stretch

With newfound energy, we threw ourselves into the project. The months flew by, and the project took shape beautifully. We incorporated Jeevan's idea, and it sparked vigor in all of us. As the work flowed, we collaborated seamlessly, supporting one another through the final touches.

When the project handover day arrived, the energy was palpable. We gathered in the specially erected event venue, our nerves mixed with excitement. As the handover process began, each one of us shared our work with excitement, showcasing everything we had accomplished. The client also responded positively and overwhelmingly. They loved our progress and commitment. They also praised our collaboration, support, and camaraderie.

A Missed Opportunity

Despite the success, once the handover meeting ended, the team was quickly reallotted to other projects. I couldn't shake the feeling that something was off. Yes, we had achieved something great, but we hadn't taken a moment to celebrate.

That night, as I drove home, I reflected on the months of hard work and the journey we had been on together. I thought about the late nights, the hard work, the brainstorming sessions, and the laughter we had shared. We had overcome significant obstacles and emerged victorious. Yet, we were already racing to the next project, and I felt a sense of sadness about how fleeting our victory felt.

Finding a Way to Celebrate

The following week, I decided to take action. I organized a *'Celebration Lunch'* at a popular restaurant for the entire team. I sent out a casual invite, hoping everyone could take a break from the office and enjoy each other's company.

On the day of the lunch, we gathered around a long table filled with delicious food. As we ate, I took a moment to reflect on our journey. I shared my gratitude for each team member's contribution, from Jeevan's innovative idea to everyone's late-night efforts. The atmosphere shifted as I spoke. Colleagues started sharing their favorite memories from the project – moments of laughter, frustration, and teamwork.

As we reminisced, I could see the pride in everyone's eyes. It was as if a weight had lifted. We were celebrating not just the successful project but the journey we had taken together. The lunch turned into a joyous occasion filled with laughter, stories, and recognition.

Effect of Celebration

In the months that followed, I noticed a profound change in our teams' contribution to their new projects. They were more engaged, collaborative, and motivated. Celebrating our success strengthened bonds and helped us recognize the value of hard work. It reminded us that achievements are not just about the end results but also about the experiences we share along the way.

Furthermore, our Vice President took note of the positive shift in morale and implemented regular recognition practices, encouraging others to celebrate their successes – both big and small. Our organization began to foster a culture of appreciation, where acknowledging each other became part of our everyday routine.

Today, I realized how important it is to celebrate success. It's easy to get caught up in the rush of work and overlook our achievements, but taking the time to acknowledge them is crucial. Celebrations create a sense of belonging, reinforce positive behaviors, and motivate us to keep pushing forward.

So, the next time you or your team accomplish something, take a moment to celebrate. It doesn't have to be grand. Sometimes, a simple gathering to share stories and laughter can have the most profound impact. Let's remember that while reaching our goals is essential, the journey we take together is what truly makes those successes meaningful.

'Recognition is not a scarce resource. You can't use it up or run out of it. The more you give it away, the more it comes back to you.' – Dan Zadra

21.

Dealing with Difficult Coworkers

In a world where tensions rise and fall,
We navigate the storms, we stand tall.
With patience as our guiding light,
We find the strength to face the fight.
Through every challenge, we will grow,
Transforming hurdles into pathways we sow.

'Difficult roads often lead to beautiful destinations.' – Zig Ziglar.

Navigating workplace dynamics can be tricky, and dealing with difficult coworkers is one of the biggest challenges most of us face at some point. Whether someone's being uncooperative, overly critical, or simply challenging to work with, these situations can be exhausting and impact everything from our productivity to our mental well-being. Learning how to handle difficult personalities effectively is essential for transforming these *'workplace hurdles'* into personal and professional growth.

In my early years working as a project manager, I faced a challenging situation with a colleague. Let me call him Manju. Manju was bright and knowledgeable but seemed determined to make every project a battle of wills. He was openly critical of others' ideas, slow to respond to emails (unless they directly impacted him), and frequently showed a dismissive attitude during team meetings.

I remember a specific incident where we were working on a big proposal for a potential client. I had gathered information from different departments and put together a draft that required input from Manju. When he finally reviewed it, he dismissed my work without even looking at it in detail, saying, *'This is far from what they will want.'* I was frustrated – my work felt undervalued, and the time crunch was real. But this experience, as challenging as it was, taught me valuable lessons about dealing with difficult personalities effectively.

Let's walk through some strategies to manage these types of situations, from understanding the types of difficult personalities to handling conflicts with professionalism and maintaining your peace of mind.

Recognize the Type of Difficult Personality You are Dealing With

Understanding the type of challenging personality, you are facing is the first step in handling the situation effectively. There are generally a few types you will encounter:

- **The Uncooperative Colleague:** They may ignore emails, fail to follow through on tasks, or show up unprepared. Working with them feels like pulling teeth, and you often find yourself covering for their lack of involvement.
- **The Overly Critical Coworker:** This person rarely has a positive thing to say and seems to nitpick everything. They might make you feel like your work is never good enough, which can be incredibly demoralizing.
- **The Know-It-All:** This type of person believes their way is the only right way and can't seem to accept anyone else's input. They often dismiss others' ideas and might monopolize conversations, leaving little room for collaboration.
- **The Passive-Aggressive** Personality: This person avoids direct confrontation but subtly undermines

others through snide remarks or withholding information. Dealing with them can feel like navigating a minefield because you are never quite sure what to expect.

Identifying the type of complex personality can help you choose a practical approach. Once I realized that Manju was the *'overly critical'* type, I knew I needed strategies to prevent his negativity from affecting my performance and morale.

Set Boundaries and Manage Expectations

Setting clear boundaries can be challenging, especially in a work setting, but it's necessary to maintain professionalism and protect your mental health. With Manju, I realized I had to be upfront about timelines and expectations. If I needed input from him, I started setting specific deadlines. I asked for his feedback in writing to minimize misunderstandings and reduce opportunities for last-minute criticism.

When dealing with an uncooperative or overly critical coworker, here are some boundary-setting tactics that may help:

- **Be Direct and Clear** in Communication: Set explicit expectations for deadlines and responsibilities. Document requests and agreements in writing whenever possible, as this can be useful if issues escalate.

- **Limit Personal Conversations:** If the coworker's attitude tends to drain you, keep interactions focused on work tasks. Reducing the time spent on small talk can help maintain a professional distance.
- **Practice Assertiveness:** It's okay to say, *'I don't have the bandwidth for that right now,'* if a colleague's requests are unreasonable or if they're making unconstructive demands.

By setting boundaries, you are not only protecting yourself but also indirectly showing the other person what you are willing to tolerate. Boundaries help maintain a respectful and productive environment, no matter how challenging the other person may be.

Use Empathy and Seek to Understand Their Perspective

As frustrating as it can be to work with challenging personalities, sometimes trying to understand their motivations and triggers can help ease tensions. Challenging behaviors are often rooted in personal insecurities, previous work experiences, or external pressures.

For example, Manju's critical nature, as I later learned, stemmed from his perfectionist tendencies and his fear of failure. Understanding this didn't excuse his behavior, but it helped me see that his dismissiveness wasn't necessarily personal – it was more about his high standards and insecurities.

When dealing with difficult personalities:

- **Ask Open-Ended Questions:** When you feel resistance, try saying something like, *'Could you help me understand your perspective on this?'* or *'Is there something specific you would like to see done differently?'* This shows you are open to dialogue and helps build mutual respect.
- **Acknowledge Their Contributions** (Even if they're small): Recognizing even minor contributions can go a long way in building rapport with critical or uncooperative colleagues.
- **Don't Assume It's About You:** People's behaviors are influenced by factors beyond what we see. Keeping this in mind helps prevent you from taking their actions personally. It allows you to approach situations with a more evident mindset.

Empathy doesn't mean you have to agree with or like everything about the person. It simply helps you see their perspective, making it easier to navigate complicated interactions without letting them affect your emotions too profoundly.

Manage Your Own Responses

One of the most empowering lessons I learned from dealing with Manju was that I couldn't control his behavior, but I could control my response to it. Practicing self-management is essential in preserving your mental well-being and professionalism in such situations.

Here's how to keep your reactions in check:

- **Take a Pause Before** Reacting: If a colleague makes a hurtful or critical comment, pause before responding. Give yourself time to process it calmly rather than reacting emotionally.
- **Focus on Solutions,** Not Problems: Reframe your mindset from focusing on how difficult a colleague is to how you can work around the challenge. In Manju's case, I started preparing more detailed drafts to reduce the likelihood of sweeping criticisms, and it minimized friction between us.
- **Practice Self-Care:** Dealing with difficult personalities can be draining, so be sure to replenish your energy. Whether it's taking a walk, talking with a trusted friend, or spending time on a hobby, self-care keeps you grounded and better prepared to face challenges.

By managing your own responses, you are not only protecting your well-being but also demonstrating professionalism and emotional resilience.

Know When to Seek Support

In some cases, especially if a problematic coworker's behavior borders on bullying or harassment, it's essential to seek support from management or HR. Document instances of unprofessional behavior, as it will provide concrete examples if the situation requires intervention. Seeking support is about creating a healthy and respectful workplace, not about blaming or *'tattling.'*

During my time with Manju, there was a point when his criticism crossed a line, and I decided to approach our manager to discuss my concerns. I was transparent, citing specific examples without exaggeration, and this allowed our manager to step in and mediate.

Knowing when to ask for help shows that you prioritize a respectful work environment, and it also reminds others of the importance of professionalism.

Final Thoughts

Working with difficult personalities isn't easy, but it can be a powerful growth experience. Each challenging coworker you encounter helps you strengthen your boundaries, improve your communication, and build resilience. Reflecting on my experience with Manju, I am grateful for the lessons I learned–they not only helped me work better with others but also helped me understand my own strengths and limits.

By approaching difficult coworkers with empathy, setting clear boundaries, and managing your responses, you can transform frustrating situations into opportunities for growth. Remember, you may not be able to change a coworker's behavior, but you can certainly control how it affects you. And ultimately, that's the real key to turning workplace hurdles into heights worth celebrating.

'We cannot control the behavior of others, but we can control our response to it.' – Unknown.

22.

Handling Constructive (and Not-So-Constructive) Feedback

In shadows cast by words unkind,
Seeds of wisdom we may find.
With open hearts, we learn to see,
The strength in truth, the chance to be.
Through storms of doubt, our roots will thrive,
In feedback's light, we come alive.

'Feedback is the breakfast of champions.' – Ken Blanchard.

Feedback affects all of us at some point in our careers. Whether it's constructive or not-so-constructive, feedback can either be a stepping stone to success or a stumbling block. So, how do we navigate this often tricky terrain?

We will explore how to take feedback on board, even when it's tough to hear, and how to effectively filter out the unhelpful criticism that can cloud our judgment.

The Value of Feedback

Feedback is an essential part of our personal and professional growth. It helps us recognize our strengths and identify areas for improvement.

Think of feedback as a map. When we're lost, a good map provides direction and shows us the path to our destination. But just like any tool, its effectiveness depends on how we use it.

In my own journey, I remember receiving feedback that shook me to my core. In my mid-career, I had a manager who had a no-nonsense approach to performance reviews. One day, after a project completion I had put my heart into, he told me, *'You need to work on your public speaking skills. You are knowledgeable, but you come off as nervous and unsure.'*

At first, I felt defensive. *'How could he not see how much effort I put in?'* I thought. It stung, and I left the meeting feeling defeated. But as I reflected on his words, I realized he had a point. My delivery could improve, and this was something I could work on.

The Importance of Self-Reflection

When we receive feedback – especially the tough kind – it's essential to take a step back and engage in self-reflection. This process involves evaluating the feedback objectively and considering its validity. Here are some questions to guide your reflection:

— **Is there a pattern?**

If multiple people mention a similar issue, it might be worth examining.

— **Is the feedback specific?**

Vague criticism often lacks substance. If someone says, *'You need to do better,'* it's harder to act on that. Seek clarity if necessary.

— **How does it align with my goals?**

Consider whether the feedback helps you move toward your personal or professional objectives.

In my case, after some reflection, I decided to take my manager's feedback seriously. I enrolled in a public speaking course, practiced in front of friends, and even recorded myself to analyze my body language. The more I worked on it, the more confident I became.

Knowing When to Embrace Feedback

Embracing feedback, especially constructive criticism, can lead to significant improvements.

Here's how to do it:

1. Listen actively

When someone gives you feedback, try to absorb it without jumping to defend yourself. Take notes if it helps.

2. Ask clarifying questions

If something isn't clear, don't hesitate to ask for specifics. This shows that you value the feedback and are eager to learn.

3. Consider the source

Understanding who is giving you the feedback can help contextualize it. A mentor's insights might carry more weight than a peer's opinion, but both can provide valuable perspectives.

One time, a colleague gave me feedback on a project I was leading. She pointed out that while the overall idea was solid, my approach could use more structure. At first, I felt a twinge of annoyance, but then I realized she was right. I thanked her for her honesty and revised the project plan. The final outcome was much more robust, and it led to greater team collaboration and outcome.

Filtering Out the Noise

Now, let's talk about the flip side: not-so-constructive feedback. We've all faced criticism that felt harsh, unhelpful, or even downright rude.

Here's how to filter out the noise:

1. **Separate the emotion from the message**

If feedback feels personal or harsh, it's easy to dismiss it entirely. Instead, try to pull out any valuable insights without letting your feelings cloud your judgment.

2. **Don't take it personally**

Sometimes, feedback reflects more about the giver than the recipient. If someone is having a bad day, their comments may be less about you and more about their struggles.

3. **Look for the intention**

If the feedback is meant to help, it's worth considering, even if it's delivered poorly. But if it feels malicious, it's okay to disregard it.

For instance, In my early career, I once received feedback from a senior executive that felt overly critical. They said, *'Your work isn't up to par with what we expect.'* I felt disheartened, but after a moment, I realized I needed to look past the harsh delivery. I reached out to my supervisor, who helped me understand specific areas where I could improve and supported me in developing a plan.

Moving Forward: A Feedback Mindset

To truly benefit from feedback, cultivating a feedback mindset is essential. This involves seeing feedback as an opportunity for growth rather than a personal attack. Here are a few tips for fostering this mindset:

1. **Reframe your thinking**

Instead of saying, *'I can't believe they criticized me,'* try, *'What can I learn from this?'* This simple shift can change your entire perspective.

2. **Seek feedback proactively**

Don't wait for performance reviews or meetings. Ask for feedback regularly from peers and mentors. This shows that you are committed to growth and improvement.

3. **Celebrate progress**

Acknowledge your improvements and successes along the way. This builds confidence and encourages you to embrace feedback even more.

Your Journey with Feedback

Navigating feedback can be a challenging journey, but it's also an incredibly rewarding one. Whether it's constructive or not-so-constructive, remember that feedback is a tool – an opportunity to grow, refine your skills, and ultimately reach new heights in your career.

As you move forward, think back to my experience and those questions I shared. Keep your heart open, filter out the noise, and embrace the learning journey that comes with feedback. After all, every piece of feedback, good or bad, is a stepping stone to your next big achievement.

'Criticism, like rain, should be gentle enough to nourish a man's growth without destroying his roots.' – Frank A. Clark.

23.

Setting Boundaries Without Seeming Uncooperative

In the dance of work, we weave our way,
Balancing needs, come what may.
With gentle words, we set the line,
Protecting our peace while still being kind.
Boundaries drawn, respect in sight,
Together we rise, in shared light.

'Boundaries are the silent guardians of our time and energy, allowing us to thrive in collaboration while safeguarding our well-being.'

Setting boundaries is a bit like walking a tightrope. On one side, we have our need for personal time and mental space. On the other, we want to maintain that collaborative, team-oriented vibe at work. So, how do we strike that balance?

Why Boundaries Matter

First off, let's chat about why boundaries are so crucial. Picture this: you are at your desk, focused on a project with a looming deadline. Suddenly, a colleague pops in to discuss their ideas. While you want to support them, you also know that this interruption could derail your entire day. This scenario is not just a one-off. It happens all the time. Without boundaries, we risk burnout, increased stress, and, ultimately, a drop in productivity.

I remember a time early in my career when I was a project coordinator. My team was tight-knit, and we often brainstormed together. However, I found myself constantly pulled into discussions that, while interesting, were sidetracking me from my tasks. I would nod and smile, wanting to be the team player, but my workload was piling up, and I felt drained.

The Fine Line of Collaboration

Setting boundaries doesn't mean we have to be the *'no'* person or appear uncooperative. Instead, think of it as a way to create a healthier work environment for everyone. When you have clear boundaries, you can contribute more effectively to discussions and projects without feeling overwhelmed.

1. Communicate Clearly and Kindly

One of the best ways to establish boundaries is through open and transparent communication. It doesn't have to be a grand speech, often, a simple statement can do wonders. For instance, if a colleague approaches you with a request, you might say, *'I would love to help, but I am currently focused on this project. Can we set a time later to discuss your ideas?'*

This approach shows that you care while also protecting your time. It's about asserting your needs without dismissing others. You can still be collaborative while ensuring your priorities are addressed.

2. Prioritize Your Tasks

Before diving into work each day, take a few moments to assess your tasks. What's urgent? What's important? Having a clear priority list not only helps you stay on track but also provides a natural excuse for saying no to non-essential requests.

I recall a particularly hectic week when my manager asked if I could take on another project. Instead of simply agreeing, I evaluated my current workload. I explained, *'I am already committed to two major projects this week, and I want to ensure I deliver quality work. Can we discuss this again next week?'* This not only showcased my commitment to quality but also provided space for planning rather than rushing through multiple tasks.

3. Set Specific Times for Collaboration

If your job requires frequent collaboration, establish specific times for meetings or brainstorming sessions. This gives everyone a clear understanding of when they can reach out and helps you manage your time more effectively.

In my experience, I found that setting aside one afternoon each week for team meetings significantly improved my workflow. I was able to plan my week around that time and dedicated my other hours to focused work. This way, my colleagues knew when to expect me to be available, and I could concentrate better without the constant interruptions.

4. Practice Saying No

Ah, the *'N'* word. It can feel daunting, but it's an essential tool in your boundary-setting arsenal. Remember, saying no doesn't have to be harsh. Instead, frame it positively. For example, *'I can't take that on right now, but I would love to help you find someone who can.'* This keeps the collaboration spirit alive while allowing you to protect your time.

A personal situation comes to mind, during a hectic quarter, a colleague approached me about leading a new initiative. I could feel the pressure to say yes, but I paused and said, *'I truly appreciate the offer, but my plate is full right now. I don't think I can give this the attention it deserves.'*

Surprisingly, they understood and even appreciated my honesty.

The Long-Term Benefits of Boundaries

When you set boundaries, you are not just protecting yourself. You are also fostering a healthier workplace culture. Team members will see your commitment to quality work and may feel empowered to establish their own boundaries. It's a ripple effect that benefits everyone.

Building Professional Relationships

Another important aspect is ensuring that your boundaries don't come across as isolation. Building and maintaining professional relationships is critical. Try to engage in casual conversations, join team lunches, or participate in collaborative projects when time allows. This demonstrates that while you are committed to your own work, you also value your relationships with your colleagues.

Real-Life Example: A Balancing Act

Let's bring this all together with a real-life example from my own journey. I once worked in a fast-paced office where the culture thrived on constant collaboration. While I enjoyed the camaraderie, I often found myself overwhelmed by the influx of ideas and requests. I realized that I needed to take control of my schedule.

I started by implementing *'office hours'* – specific times each week when my colleagues could come to me with their ideas or questions. This way, I could focus on my tasks without feeling guilty about shutting the door. Not only did this give me the breathing room I needed, but it also encouraged my coworkers to come prepared with their thoughts, making our meetings more productive.

Every time, my colleagues respected my boundaries and even started implementing similar practices. We all learned to value our individual time while still maintaining a collaborative environment.

Final Thoughts

Setting boundaries at work doesn't mean you have to be uncooperative or disengaged. Instead, it's about finding that sweet spot where you can protect your time and energy while still being a valuable team member. Remember, it's all in how you communicate your needs and how you prioritize your work.

So, the next time you feel overwhelmed, take a step back, evaluate your boundaries, and don't hesitate to assert them. You will be surprised at how much more productive and fulfilled you will feel. After all, we're all in this together, striving for heights we can reach, and a little balance can go a long way!

'By setting boundaries with grace, we empower ourselves and our teams to reach new heights, fostering a culture of respect and collaboration.'

24.

Managing Up

To manage up is a thoughtful art,
Aligning minds, yet staying apart.
We bridge the gaps, adapt with grace,
Finding strength in a shared space.
With trust as the seed, success will grow,
Turning hurdles to heights as we go.

'Success in any job hinges not just on doing your work well, but on understanding the people around you – especially the ones leading you.'

It's easy to think that success depends solely on doing your job well, focusing on the tasks at hand, and working hard to achieve individual goals. But anyone who's spent even a little time in the workplace knows that there's another side to success: understanding and adapting to the people around you. This is especially true when it comes to your relationship with your manager.

'Managing up' is the skill of adapting to your manager's work style, preferences, and expectations so you can build a productive, harmonious working relationship. This isn't about manipulating or simply trying to please your manager. Instead, it's a proactive approach to ensure you are on the same page, working in sync, and achieving shared goals. Think of it as learning a new language – one where you speak in a way that resonates with the person leading you. Not only does it foster better communication and productivity, but it also opens up doors to more trust, autonomy, and opportunities.

Let's dive into some core elements of 'Managing up' effectively, including a personal example that helped me understand the impact of this approach.

Understanding Your Manager's Work Style

One of the first steps in 'Managing up' is understanding your manager's work style. Each of us has a unique way of approaching tasks, solving problems, and communicating.

Managers are no exception, and they often have strong preferences based on what's worked for them in the past.

Some managers are detail-oriented and thrive on having all the information before making a decision. They want frequent updates, detailed reports, and thorough explanations. Others prefer a high-level summary and might even get bogged down by too many details. And some managers value face-to-face conversations over email. In contrast, others prefer a well-organized inbox and minimal in-person interruptions.

Knowing your manager's style can significantly impact your day-to-day interactions. For example, if you are working for someone who values a detail-oriented approach, sending brief emails might leave them feeling like they don't have enough information. On the other hand, an executive who prefers summaries may appreciate short, punchy updates.

Take the time to observe how your manager communicates with others, how they structure their workday, and how they make decisions. If you are unsure, don't hesitate to ask subtle questions to clarify their preferences. Even a quick, *'Would you prefer a weekly summary, or should I send updates as things come up?'* shows that you are paying attention and willing to adapt.

Adapting to Their Preferences and Expectations

Once you have a handle on your manager's work style, it's time to adapt to their preferences and expectations. This isn't about losing your own voice or ignoring your own needs – it's about finding a balance that works for both of you.

During one of the years in my career, I worked under a manager who was an extremely early bird. She liked to start her workday at 7a.m. sharp and was usually the most focused during those first couple of hours. Naturally, she expected our team to be highly responsive to her emails and questions during that time. At first, this was challenging for me, as I preferred starting my day a bit later and felt more productive in the late morning. However, I quickly realized that by not adapting to her preferred schedule, I was missing opportunities to get feedback, clarify questions, and move projects forward during the time she was most attentive.

So, I made a change. I began to shift my schedule, starting work earlier to align with her prime hours. I didn't necessarily have to work more hours, but moving my focus time to align with hers made a noticeable difference. My manager started to recognize my commitment and responsiveness, and our working relationship improved. She also became more open to allowing me flexible time for other parts of my day because she saw that I was willing to make adjustments to align with her needs. This experience taught me that sometimes, creating a slight shift in your approach can have a significant impact on your professional relationships.

Building Trust Through Proactive Communication

'Managing up' also involves building trust, which is often achieved through proactive communication. This means anticipating your manager's questions, concerns, and feedback before they even arise. Rather than waiting to be asked for updates, provide them ahead of time. If a project might face delays, let your manager know as soon as possible instead of waiting until the deadline.

For example, if you know your manager is concerned about a particular project milestone, don't wait for the weekly check-in to bring up issues or roadblocks. Instead, reach out to them with a quick email update to let them know where things stand. This type of proactive communication demonstrates that you are on top of things, organized and that you care about the project as much as they do.

Not only does this build trust, but it also positions you as a reliable problem-solver rather than someone who only raises concerns after they become issues. Your manager will appreciate your initiative and begin to see you as someone they can rely on to keep things on track.

Learning Their Priorities and Vision

Every manager has priorities and a vision for their team, department, or even the entire organization. Understanding this *'big picture'* is essential to 'Managing up' effectively. When you know what your manager values and the direction they want to head, it's much easier to align your work with their goals.

Ask yourself, what are the issues that keep my manager up at night? What metrics or projects seem to get their most focused attention? If you are not sure, ask. A simple question like, *'What's the most important goal for our team this quarter?'* or *'What would success look like for you on this project?'* can open up a conversation that allows you to align your work more closely with their vision.

When you tailor your efforts to match their priorities, you not only make your manager's job easier, but you also position yourself as a strategic thinker who can look beyond individual tasks. And as an added benefit, this will often lead to more recognition, responsibility, and advancement opportunities.

Establishing Boundaries

While 'Managing up' often requires flexibility, it's also crucial to establish healthy boundaries. Flexibility doesn't mean being available 24/7 or changing your style to the point that it compromises your well-being. It's about communicating in a way that's clear, respectful, and maintains your personal boundaries.

For example, work with a manager who tends to send emails late at night or over the weekend. It can be tempting to respond immediately to show your commitment.

However, unless this is part of your team's culture or expected work style, it's okay to set boundaries. You might communicate by saying, *'I will make sure to address these emails first thing in the morning.'* Setting expectations like this can prevent misunderstandings, burnout, and ultimately help you maintain a healthy work-life balance.

The Benefits of 'Managing up'

The rewards of 'Managing up' are well worth the effort. When you understand and align with your manager's preferences, you create a smoother, more enjoyable working relationship. Over time, you will likely find that your manager trusts you more, gives you greater autonomy, and may even seek your input on important decisions.

In my own experience, making that small shift to accommodate my manager's early hours led not only to a better working relationship but also opened up more responsibility and leadership opportunities for me. Because I took the initiative to understand her needs, she began to see me as a reliable partner. That trust made her more comfortable delegating high-impact projects to me.

Wrapping Up

'Managing up' is not about compromising your identity or becoming someone, you are not. It's about learning to navigate and work with different personalities in a way that benefits everyone involved.

By understanding your manager's work style, adapting to their preferences, building trust through proactive communication, aligning with their priorities, and setting healthy boundaries, you create a solid foundation for success.

Consider this skill as an essential component of your professional toolkit. The ability to 'Manage up' not only enhances your effectiveness but also builds relationships and opens doors that may have otherwise remained closed.

It's one of the best ways to turn workplace hurdles into heights, helping you – and your team – reach new levels of success.

'Managing up isn't about pleasing, it's about partnering – aligning your strengths with your manager's vision to create something greater together.'

25.

Balancing Competing Priorities

Juggling tasks like a dance on a wire,
Projects and deadlines, demands never tire.
Yet with focus and heart, the chaos refines,
Turning each hurdle to heights we define.
Balance the load, let quality soar–
This is the art of giving your core.

'Priorities are not about choosing what to do, they're about choosing what not to let go.'

Balancing Competing Priorities is the art of Managing the Juggle without Losing Your Edge.

If you have ever felt like there's too much to do and not enough time, you are not alone. Modern workplaces demand a lot from us, with projects, deadlines, and requests flying in from all directions. Balancing these demands without sacrificing quality can feel like an impossible feat – like juggling three balls while someone keeps tossing in more. But with the right strategies, you can manage multiple priorities effectively and still produce great work.

This chapter dives into how to manage competing priorities, drawing from real-life experiences to illustrate what works (and what doesn't). Let's get into some practical strategies to handle this with less stress and more confidence.

Why Balancing Competing Priorities is Harder Than It Seems

Balancing priorities isn't just about managing time, it's about managing energy, focus, and resources, too. When several projects overlap or when multiple stakeholders want attention at once, it's easy to feel overwhelmed. Each task has its own weight and level of importance, yet we often try to give each the same amount of attention. That can lead to burnout, mistakes, and frustration.

One real-life experience from my career stands out. A few years ago, I was handling three big projects at once, all of which had critical deadlines and visible results. One project required regular coordination with an external team, and another demanded technical expertise that I needed to brush up on. The third was an internal initiative with a tight timeline and daily check-ins with the executive team. Each project was necessary, and all three had different leaders who understandably wanted high-quality results.

That experience taught me a lot about how to stay organized, communicate clearly, and set boundaries – all essential tools for managing competing priorities. Here's what I learned and how you can apply it to your work.

1. Prioritize by Impact, Not Just Urgency

When everything feels urgent, it's hard to see what's actually essential. A common mistake is to respond to the loudest voice first, but the most pressing task isn't always the most valuable.

Start by evaluating each task's impact. Think about these questions:

- What's the worst-case scenario if this doesn't get done on time?
- How does this contribute to my or my team's overall goals?
- Who will be affected, and how much influence do they have?

In my case, I had to look at each of my three projects and honestly assess which would have the most significant impact. The executive team's project took priority because it was foundational for future work and involved decision-makers. By focusing on that project first each day, I was able to create momentum without feeling like I was putting out fires.

2. Set Clear Boundaries and Expectations with Stakeholders

Having competing priorities means multiple people may have different expectations of your time and results. It's crucial to communicate openly with each stakeholder so they know what to expect from you and when.

For instance, when working with the external team on one of my projects, I had to be upfront about the limits of my availability due to the other two priorities. I scheduled regular update meetings to provide a consistent flow of communication and reassure them that the project was on track. Knowing they'd get regular updates helped me manage their expectations and gave me space to focus on other projects without constant interruptions.

Remember, it's okay to say, *'Here's what I can commit to,'* rather than over-promising. This builds trust and ensures stakeholders know you are committed while also juggling other responsibilities.

3. Use Time Blocks to Maximize Focus

Switching from one project to another constantly can kill productivity. Every time we switch, we lose a little focus and efficiency, and it's exhausting to continually recalibrate our brains.

A lifesaver for me was using time blocking. Each day, I would block off specific periods dedicated to one project, even if it was just 30 minutes. During those blocks, I would focus only on the assigned project. I avoided emails, phone calls, or anything else unless it was critical.

For example:

- Morning Block: Executive team project updates and planning.
- Midday Block: Collaboration with the external team on project milestones.
- Afternoon Block: Skill-building and technical deep-dive for the third project.

This approach helped me make significant progress on each project without feeling pulled in too many directions. Plus, it allowed me to mentally *'switch gears'* between tasks instead of constantly multitasking, which ultimately improved the quality of my work.

4. Delegate and Share Responsibilities Where Possible

When competing priorities pile up, there's a tendency to want to handle everything yourself. However, effective delegation can be a powerful tool to help you meet deadlines and maintain quality.

During my three-project scenario, I realized that some tasks, while important, didn't necessarily require my specific input. I delegated a few administrative tasks to a junior team member. I shared responsibility with a peer for some reporting duties on the internal initiative. By doing this, I freed up my time for higher-impact work.

When delegating, be clear about the tasks, timelines, and expectations, and ensure the person taking them on has the resources they need. Delegation doesn't mean offloading responsibility, it means trusting others to contribute and empowering them to do their best.

5. Schedule Regular Reviews and Adjust as Needed

Projects evolve, and priorities can shift quickly. Suppose you are not consistently reviewing your progress and the relative importance of each task. In that case, you might find yourself investing energy where it's no longer needed.

For me, a weekly review of my priorities was essential. Every Friday, I would assess where I was with each project, noting any changing timelines or shifting needs. This helped me see when one project could take a backseat or when another needed more immediate attention. Adjusting regularly helped me stay on top of all three projects without feeling overwhelmed by unexpected changes.

It's easy to fall into a reactive mode, but setting aside time to review and adjust is a proactive way to handle competing priorities.

6. Learn to Say *'No'* or *'Not Right Now'*

Sometimes, you can't take on more without compromising quality. Learning to say *'no'* or *'not right now'* is a critical skill. It's tough, especially if you are worried about how others might perceive you. However, saying *'yes'* to everything can lead to burnout or incomplete work.

When I was balancing those three projects, there were several occasions when additional tasks came my way. After assessing my bandwidth, I had to politely decline a couple of smaller requests, explaining that I would be able to give them my full attention once these projects were in a steadier state. Most people appreciated the honesty and were willing to wait. In the end, saying *'no'* allowed me to deliver better results for each project I committed to.

Balancing for the Long Term

Balancing competing priorities isn't about finding a magic formula, it's about staying adaptable and aware. Not every day will go perfectly, and there will be times when you feel stretched too thin. But by prioritizing impact, setting clear expectations, time-blocking, delegating, reviewing progress, and saying *'no'* when necessary, you will find yourself managing the juggle with more confidence and less stress.

Remember, the goal isn't just to get through each project, it's to grow from each experience. Every time you balance priorities, you gain skills and insights that make you more effective and resilient. And that's what turns hurdles into heights.

Balancing multiple demands will always be a challenge. But with these strategies, you will be equipped to take on any workload without compromising the quality of your work or burning out. After all, balancing priorities isn't just about meeting deadlines, it's about doing it in a way that allows you to thrive, not just survive.

'True balance isn't about giving everything equal time–it's about giving the right things your best time.'

26.

Finding a Mentor

In the shadows, wisdom glows,
A mentor's voice, where courage grows.
With gentle guidance, paths align,
While sponsors lift, their trust divine.
Together, they pave the way ahead,
To heights untold, where dreams are fed.

'Mentorship is the bridge between where you are and where you want to be, sponsorship is the push that gets you across.'

If you are aiming for growth in your career, identifying the right mentors and sponsors is one of the smartest moves you can make. Mentors are like trusted advisors – they help guide your development, offer advice, and act as sounding boards. Sponsors, on the other hand, are advocates within your organization or industry who can vouch for you and create opportunities that push you forward.

In this chapter, let's explore why both mentors and sponsors matter and how you can find and nurture these relationships. I will even share a story from my own journey to illustrate just how impactful the right support can be.

Why Mentors and Sponsors Are Essential

Think about someone you admire in your field or organization. Chances are, they didn't make it to their current position solely through hard work. At some point, they likely had a mentor guiding them or a sponsor advocating on their behalf, helping them climb higher and overcome challenges.

1. **Mentors** are there to support and guide you. They will listen, offer advice, and give you honest feedback when you need it. A mentor could help you refine your skills, navigate tricky situations, or build confidence.

2. **Sponsors** have a different, more public role in your career. They don't just give advice, they actively use their influence to endorse you and put you forward for opportunities, promotions, or high-visibility projects.

So, while mentors are invaluable for personal and professional growth, sponsors are essential for making significant career moves. But both are necessary in your journey toward success.

How to Identify a Mentor

Finding a mentor doesn't mean approaching the most senior person in your company. Often, the best mentors are those who are just a few steps ahead of you in their careers. They have a clear understanding of your current challenges and are familiar with the stepping stones to the next level.

1. Look for Alignment in Values and Career Goals

The ideal Mentor is someone whose values and career goals resonate with you. This alignment makes for a natural connection, as they will understand what drives you. Think about someone in your network or company whose work you admire and who has a reputation for being helpful and generous with their time.

2. Observe Potential Mentors in Action

Before reaching out to potential mentors, observe them to see how they interact with others. Are they approachable, supportive, and patient? It's important that they're genuinely interested in helping others succeed, as this will impact the quality of the mentoring relationship.

3. Don't Limit Yourself to One Mentor

You can have multiple mentors for different areas of your life. For example, you might seek a mentor in your industry to improve your technical skills and another within your company to learn the organizational culture. A diverse network of mentors can provide a richer perspective and support across various aspects of your career.

My Own Journey with Mentorship

When I was starting out in my career, I met someone who ended up being a fantastic mentor. Let's call her Sita. I was new to the industry and felt a bit lost, navigating the complexities of the job and understanding the politics of a large organization. Sita was about ten years ahead of me in her career and had a lot of insight into the dynamics of the company.

One day, I asked her for feedback on a project I would been working on. She took the time to walk me through what I did well and where I could improve, but she also encouraged me to see things from a strategic angle. *'Think beyond the immediate task,'* she said. *'How does this project fit into the bigger picture? And how can you position yourself as an asset in that context?'*

Those words shifted my perspective entirely. From that point on, Sita became my sounding board for various decisions, and her insights helped me grow in ways I hadn't anticipated. More importantly, her feedback gave me the confidence to advocate for myself and take on more responsibilities.

How to Find a Sponsor

While a mentor can guide you, a sponsor can open doors. In many cases, your sponsor might be a senior leader or influential figure who recognizes your potential and is willing to put their credibility on the line to support you.

1. Demonstrate Your Value First

Before you can find a sponsor, you need to prove yourself. Sponsors are usually busy people with significant influence, so they need to see that you are committed, reliable, and capable of delivering results. Consistently doing great work, being proactive, and showing initiative will get you noticed and lay the foundation for sponsorship.

2. Be Vocal About Your Ambitions

While mentors will often guide you toward your goals, sponsors need to know you are ready for the next step. Make sure that senior leaders and influential people within your network are aware of your career aspirations. Please don't assume they know you want to advance, instead, communicate your goals clearly and respectfully.

3. Seek Opportunities to Work Closely with Potential Sponsors

One effective way to gain a sponsor is by volunteering for high-profile projects where senior leaders are involved. This not only puts you on their radar but also gives them the chance to see your strengths firsthand. Be proactive and take ownership, and they will start to view you as someone ready for more responsibility.

How My Sponsor Helped Shape My Career

There was a pivotal moment in my career when I was up for a promotion that I would work tirelessly to earn. However, I wasn't the only one in line for this role, and I wasn't the most experienced candidate on paper. A senior executive named Rajiv, who had observed my work on a recent project, became my unexpected sponsor.

Rajiv saw my dedication, my ability to lead, and my willingness to take on challenges. He spoke up in meetings where I wasn't present, highlighting my contributions and pushing for me to be given the role. Without his advocacy, I may not have gotten that opportunity as early in my career as I did. His support taught me the value of having a sponsor who genuinely believes in you and isn't afraid to advocate for your advancement.

Nurturing Mentor and Sponsor Relationships

Building and maintaining relationships with mentors and sponsors requires effort. Here are a few tips to nurture these connections:

1. **Show Appreciation** – Express gratitude for their guidance and support. A simple *'thank you'* or sharing how their advice helped can go a long way.

2. **Stay Engaged** – Regularly update them on your progress. They will appreciate seeing your growth and dedication, which strengthens the relationship.
3. **Offer Help When Possible** – Don't assume the relationship is one-sided. Find small ways to add value, whether that's sharing valuable resources, offering feedback on a topic of interest, or simply being a supportive contact in their network.
4. **Be Open and Honest** – Building trust is critical. Share your challenges, ask for honest feedback, and be receptive to their advice, even if it's not always what you want to hear.

Leveraging Mentors and Sponsors to Reach New Heights

Mentors and sponsors are two of the most valuable assets you can have on your career journey. Mentors guide you, offering wisdom, feedback, and the kind of support that helps you grow over time. Sponsors actively use their influence to create opportunities and vouch for your capabilities.

In my own journey, having a mentor like Sita provided me with insights and confidence. At the same time, Rajiv's sponsorship opened doors that were critical for my career advancement. The combination of both types of support turned potential hurdles into stepping stones.

As you continue in your career, remember that seeking guidance and advocacy is not a sign of weakness, it's a sign of strength and self-awareness. Finding mentors who align with your goals and sponsors who champion your potential will help you grow professionally, overcome obstacles, and reach the heights you are aiming for. Embrace these relationships, nurture them, and watch your career soar.

'Success is not just about what you know, but who you know – and how they believe in you.'

27.

Navigating Office Politics

In halls where whispers weave their thread,
Alliances form, where trust is spread.
With empathy's light, we find our way,
Through shadows of rivalry, brightening the gray.
In unity's dance, we rise and strive,
Together, we flourish, together, we thrive.

'The most successful people are those who can navigate the politics of their workplace while staying true to their values.' – Unknown.

Navigating office politics can feel like walking through a maze. It's not just about the official hierarchy or your boss's authority. It's about understanding the intricacies of relationships, alliances, and, sometimes, rivalries that exist within your workplace. When we talk about office politics, many of us think it's synonymous with manipulation or backstabbing. While those elements do exist, I like to think of office politics as the subtle dance of relationships that shapes our work environment and impacts decision-making.

The Hidden Web of Influence

At its core, understanding office politics means recognizing the informal power structures in your workplace. These structures often operate below the surface but are incredibly influential. Who gets to decide on project priorities? Who gets credit for a successful initiative? These questions are usually answered not just by those who have formal authority but by those who have the right relationships.

Think of it this way: in a corporate setting, there are usually a few key players – let's call them the *'informal leaders.'* These individuals may not have fancy titles, but their influence can be felt throughout the organization. They could be the go-to person in their department, someone with a wealth of knowledge, or even the person who always knows the latest gossip. Understanding who these individuals are and how they operate can give you a significant advantage.

Building Your Own Alliances

As you navigate this landscape, consider how you can build your own alliances. You might not have direct authority, but you can create networks of support that help you influence decisions. This doesn't mean playing a game of favoritism or being disingenuous. Instead, it's about fostering genuine relationships based on trust and mutual respect.

Once, on a significant project that required input from multiple departments. The project was crucial for my team's success, but I quickly realized that I was up against some strong personalities. One person, in particular, was known for being quite tricky and often undermined others' contributions.

Instead of trying to confront this individual head-on, I decided to seek out informal conversations with colleagues in other departments. I learned who had previously worked with this person and asked them how they approached interactions. I discovered that establishing common ground and showing respect for their expertise helped diffuse tensions. I began to frame discussions around shared goals rather than differences, and slowly but surely, I earned the respect of my peers and even my difficult colleagues.

This experience taught me a valuable lesson – often, the most effective way to navigate office politics is not by competing against others but by understanding their perspectives and aligning your goals with theirs.

The Role of Communication

Effective communication is a vital skill in navigating office politics. Being able to articulate your ideas clearly and listen to others can help you build rapport and credibility. Remember, it's not just about what you say but how you say it. Tailoring your communication style to fit the preferences of your audience can make a significant difference.

For instance, if you are presenting an idea to upper management, consider their priorities. They might be focused on cost savings, so framing your proposal in terms of financial impact can be persuasive. Conversely, when discussing ideas with your peers, a collaborative approach that seeks input and builds consensus can create a more supportive environment.

Understanding Motivations and Competing Interests

One of the critical components of office politics is understanding the varying motivations and interests that colleagues bring to the table. Each person has unique goals that influence their decisions and behaviors. When you take the time to understand these motivations, you can navigate conflicts and build alliances more effectively.

For example, consider a scenario where two teams are competing for resources. Team A believes their project is a strategic priority for the company's growth. At the same time, Team B feels equally passionate about their initiative, which focuses on improving customer satisfaction. The tension between these two teams might be palpable, and it can impact decision-making at higher levels.

In this case, instead of viewing it as a battle to win, think of it as an opportunity to find a solution that benefits everyone. Engage in conversations with members from both teams to understand their priorities. You might find that a compromise can be reached, or perhaps there's a way to incorporate elements from both projects into a larger initiative that satisfies everyone involved.

The Impact of Office Culture

Office politics also intertwines with the overall culture of an organization. In a workplace where collaboration and transparency are valued, navigating politics can feel more straightforward. Employees are more likely to engage in open communication and support one another, which can reduce the adversarial nature of office politics.

Conversely, in a culture that encourages competition and secrecy, politics can become a minefield. In such environments, employees may feel pressured to engage in cutthroat behavior, which can lead to mistrust and decreased morale.

As a leader or an employee, you can influence the workplace culture by modeling transparency and collaboration. Encourage open dialogue, provide opportunities for cross-departmental collaboration, and celebrate shared successes. When everyone feels included and valued, the negative aspects of office politics can diminish.

The Power of Empathy

One of the most underrated tools in navigating office politics is empathy. Understanding where others are coming from can help you build stronger connections. Everyone has their own pressures, goals, and challenges. By showing genuine interest in your colleagues' perspectives, you can foster a more collaborative environment.

Going back to my earlier story, I realized that my difficult colleague was under immense pressure from upper management to deliver results. By acknowledging their stress and offering support, I was able to turn a potential adversary into an ally. This not only improved our working relationship but also made the project more successful as we combined our strengths.

Strategies for Successful Navigation

Now that we've explored various aspects of office politics, let's discuss some strategies to navigate this complex landscape effectively –

1. **Observe and Learn:** Take time to understand the dynamics within your workplace. Pay attention to interactions, relationships, and decision-making processes. This insight will help you identify key players and their motivations.

2. **Build Relationships:** Invest in building genuine relationships with colleagues across different levels and departments. Networking isn't just for job searches, it's also about creating a support system within your workplace.

3. **Stay Professional:** In the face of office politics, maintain your professionalism. Avoid gossiping or engaging in harmful behavior, as this can backfire and damage your reputation.
4. **Communicate Effectively:** Tailor your communication to suit your audience. Be clear, concise, and respectful in your interactions. Listening is just as critical as speaking.
5. **Be Adaptable:** Office politics can be unpredictable. Be prepared to adjust your strategies as situations change. Flexibility is critical to navigating shifting dynamics.
6. **Seek Feedback:** Regularly seek feedback from colleagues and mentors. This not only helps you improve but also fosters open communication and collaboration.
7. **Maintain Integrity:** Always stay true to your values. Navigating office politics doesn't mean compromising your principles. Being authentic will help you build trust and credibility over time.

Final Thoughts

As you move forward in your career, keep these principles in mind. Office politics is an inevitable part of the workplace. But with a thoughtful approach, you can turn potential hurdles into stepping stones. By understanding the informal power structures, building alliances, recognizing competing interests, and communicating effectively, you will not only navigate the complexities of office politics but thrive in your professional journey. Remember, every challenge is an opportunity waiting to be seized!

'Mastering office politics is not merely about survival, it's about thriving by creating an environment where everyone can succeed.' – Unknown.

28.

Leading Without a Formal Leadership Role

You don't need a title, a badge, or a crown,
To lift others up, to never back down.
With small acts of courage, and words that inspire,
You can kindle a spark, set hearts afire.
True leaders rise where no titles are worn–
In the trust they build and the change they've sworn.

'You don't need a title to be a leader, you just need the courage to make a difference and the heart to inspire others.'

Leadership isn't reserved for people with titles. Real leadership often shines through in moments when there is no formal designation. I have learned this firsthand, and over time, I have seen that sometimes, the most influential individuals are those without any official authority. They are the ones who can guide, influence, and inspire those around them – no title is required.

So, what does it look like to lead without a title? How do you influence, inspire, and make an impact within your team or organization when you are not *'the boss'*? Let's walk through what it takes and why your influence might even be stronger than someone who does have that official role.

Why Leading Without a Title Matters

In any team, there are *'roles'* that go far beyond titles. There is the go-to person for tech issues, the morale booster, the problem-solver, and the person everyone trusts. You might notice that people gravitate towards these unofficial leaders, valuing their advice and often following their lead. So, even without an official title, you can play an essential role in how your team operates, how well it functions, and how connected people feel to each other.

People who lead without a title can offer something precious, authentic influence. They are not motivated by a job description but by a desire to make things better, to help the team succeed, and to create a positive work environment. And often, these *'title-free'* leaders can build deep, genuine relationships, which in turn builds trust – the cornerstone of any successful team.

Key Ways to Demonstrate Leadership Without a Title

1. Focus on Relationships, Not Authority

In any team, relationships are your real power base. Start by building genuine relationships. Connect with others by understanding their goals, challenges, and how you can support them. People want to feel understood, so when you show genuine interest in them and offer your help, you are setting a foundation for influence.

For instance, in a previous role, I noticed a team member, let's call him Jake, was struggling with a particular project. Though it wasn't my responsibility, I offered to help him troubleshoot. Over time, he started coming to me with questions and concerns, and soon, other team members did the same. It wasn't long before I had become a go-to person in the team, even though I had no formal authority. By simply focusing on supporting others, I became someone they trusted.

2. Be the Solution-Finder

Teams thrive on solutions, not just observations of problems. Suppose you can identify areas for improvement and contribute ideas for positive change. In that case, you will quickly become a valued team member. Solution-finders have a ripple effect on the team. They help cut down on stress and foster a proactive work environment.

In one of my projects, my team was struggling with a process that was causing delays and frustration. We all knew it was inefficient, but nobody was stepping up to tackle it. Eshwar decided to take the lead, not by overhauling everything but by asking questions and initiating small changes. Eshwar gathered feedback from the team, and we worked together to brainstorm better approaches. Over a few weeks, our process became noticeably smoother, and it was something we all took pride in. By focusing on solutions rather than merely pointing out the issues, Eshwar helped our team operate more effectively. In the process, I had a much stronger voice when future changes were needed.

3. Develop Empathy and Listen Actively

Leadership is about connecting with people on a human level, and the most effective way to do that's by truly listening. Active listening shows people that you value their perspectives, which builds trust and encourages open communication. In team settings, it's common to get wrapped up in task-focused conversations, but taking a moment to understand how others are feeling and what they're experiencing can make all the difference.

In one of my past teams, we were under a lot of pressure, and morale was low. Instead of diving right into work, I would start by checking in with team members, asking how they were doing or if they needed support. These small moments showed them I cared beyond the projects we were working on. Over time, they opened up more, and we grew into a more supportive team. This emotional connection enabled us to push through challenging times together, and we became a more cohesive unit.

4. Model the Behavior You Want to See

Actions speak louder than words, especially when you are not in a formal leadership role. Leading by example is one of the most potent ways to influence your team. Show up with a positive attitude, demonstrate accountability, and stay open to learning. When people see you practicing what you preach, they will be more likely to adopt similar behaviors.

I remember one instance when a project deadline was rapidly approaching, and everyone was feeling the heat. Instead of complaining about the timeline or stress, Veera – my Project Manager – focused on being proactive, staying late to get ahead, and keeping a positive outlook. Veera's attitude caught on, and soon, the team started mirroring that energy. By keeping his focus on what he could control and pushing forward, Veera set the tone for others, making a challenging project a little more manageable.

5. Communicate Effectively and Openly

Transparent and consistent communication is a cornerstone of leadership, title or not. Sharing information openly, explaining your ideas clearly, and listening to feedback create a more collaborative and inclusive team atmosphere. Effective communicators are natural leaders because they help everyone understand the bigger picture and build a sense of belonging.

In one role, I often worked with cross-functional teams, which meant information was scattered across different departments. Arati, a project analyst on my team, took it upon herself to bridge the communication gap, updating team members on relevant information and ensuring everyone was aligned. Even though it wasn't part of her job description, this helped build her credibility within the team, and people started relying on her as an information source. Over time, I could see how much smoother our team operated simply because we were all on the same page.

How I Saw the Impact Firsthand

I worked on a team where my managers were often pulled into other projects, leaving us somewhat directionless. I noticed that my teammates were feeling frustrated and disconnected. Rather than waiting for guidance, Karthik – a program manager – I began organizing weekly team check-ins, where he discussed progress, brainstormed solutions, and shared challenges.

Initially, it felt awkward stepping up, but my team members started looking forward to these sessions. They saw Karthik as a consistent figure in the midst of change, and he became the go-to person for coordinating efforts and keeping morale up. Though he wasn't in the driver's seat, he saw that his willingness to lead simply by bringing people together made a meaningful difference. By the time our manager returned to the project, we were more unified and had made significant progress – all because of a few simple initiatives Karthik had taken to connect and guide the team.

Practical Takeaways to Lead Without a Title

If you are ready to start leading from within, here are some practical tips to keep in mind:

1. **Engage with your team:** Ask how you can help, listen actively, and focus on strengthening those relationships.
2. **Take initiative:** Identify problems and work on solutions – don't wait for permission to make things better.
3. **Be consistent:** Show up every day with a positive attitude and a commitment to doing your best. Consistency builds trust.
4. **Seek feedback:** Ask others how you can improve and show that you value their input. This encourages a culture of openness.
5. **Share credit and acknowledge others:** Recognizing others for their contributions strengthens the team bond and reinforces trust.

Final Thoughts

Leading without a formal title is all about influence, not authority. It's about how you show up for others, how you communicate, and the attitude you bring to work. You don't need an official title to make a big difference. What matters is your willingness to step up, connect with others, and lead by example. When you focus on bringing value to your team, you will naturally become a leader, regardless of your position.

The best part? This type of leadership is often the most impactful and enduring because it's rooted in authenticity and trust.

So, go ahead, lead from where you are – and watch the difference it makes.

'True leadership isn't about authority, it's about the influence you build by lifting others and leading by example. Titles fade, but the impact of authentic leadership endures.'

29.

Managing an Overwhelming Workload

When the weight of work feels like too much to bear,
Step back, take a breath, reclaim the air.
Prioritize wisely, let go where you can,
Set firm boundaries, make space in your plan.
With balance and focus, the load feels light,
From hurdles to heights, you are ready to fight.

'You don't have to do it all, just the things that matter most.'

If you are anything like I was at one point in my career, you know the feeling all too well.

The constant barrage of emails, meetings, deadlines, and projects piling up on your desk is enough to make anyone feel on the edge. That sense of an endless to-do list can make us feel like we are treading water, barely keeping afloat.

But here's the good news: feeling overwhelmed doesn't mean we have to remain stuck. With the right tools, we can turn that pressure into productivity, protect our well-being, and ultimately achieve more with less stress. I will walk you through how I have learned to prioritize, delegate, and set boundaries. Hopefully, by the end, you will have some strategies to apply to your own life.

Understanding the Overwhelm

To put this into perspective, I take you back to a time when my workload was at its peak.

I had recently been promoted, which was an exciting new chapter in my career, but it came with additional responsibilities. I was now leading a team, managing client accounts, and still expected to deliver my own set of projects.

In my eagerness to prove myself, I was saying *'yes'* to everything. Client calls, internal meetings, after-hours email checks – you name it, I was there.

It didn't take long for the overwhelm to creep in. At first, I could handle it. Soon enough, my days blurred into one another. I was working long hours, and worst of all, my productivity actually started to drop. Despite putting in more hours, I wasn't accomplishing as much, and the quality of my work was slipping. I realized I needed a change – I had to learn how to manage my workload better or risk Burnout.

Step 1: Prioritizing Tasks Effectively

The first step to managing an overwhelming workload is understanding that not everything is urgent or equally important. I remember the moment I embraced the concept of prioritization. It was like a weight lifted off my shoulders. I realized that by trying to do everything all at once, I was spreading myself too thin, and nothing was getting my full attention. Here's a simple method that was taught to me by my mentor and that worked wonders for me –

The Eisenhower Matrix

This prioritization tool divides tasks into four categories:

1. **Urgent and Important:** These tasks need immediate attention and directly impact your goals.
2. **Important but Not Urgent:** These are important but don't need to be done immediately.
3. **Urgent but Not Important:** These tasks are often distractions or busy work.
4. **Not Urgent and Not Important:** These can be minimized or delegated.

By categorizing my tasks, I could see what truly needed my attention right now and what could wait. For example, instead of responding to every email the moment it landed in my inbox, I set specific times during the day for email checks. That way, I wasn't constantly pulled away from more critical tasks, like preparing for a major client meeting.

Daily and Weekly Task Reviews

Each day, take a few minutes in the morning to assess your most important tasks for the day. I also found that taking 10-15 minutes on Fridays to plan the upcoming week helped me start Monday with a clearer vision of what to tackle. This routine reduced the feeling of overwhelm and gave me a sense of control over my workload.

Step 2: Learning to Delegate

Delegating is a skill that often takes time to develop. I used to feel that I was responsible for every aspect of my work, and by handing off tasks, I was somehow shirking my duties. But the truth is, learning to delegate doesn't diminish your abilities – it enhances your effectiveness.

One of the most impactful lessons I learned about delegation came from a project where I was managing a tight deadline for a client presentation. I had a capable team member who offered to help. But, I hesitated to assign tasks because I wanted to ensure everything was done *'my way.'* Eventually, I was so overwhelmed that I had no choice but to accept their offer. Not only did they complete the work flawlessly, but they also added a fresh perspective to the project that improved the final presentation.

How to Delegate Effectively

- **Identify strengths and interests:** Take time to understand the skills and interests of your team members. By assigning tasks that play to their strengths, you empower them and ensure a higher-quality outcome.
- **Provide clear instructions and expectations:** Be explicit about deadlines and expectations to prevent miscommunication.
- **Trust but verify:** After assigning a task, trust your team to get it done. Check-in periodically, but avoid micromanaging. A light touch shows your team that you trust them while ensuring progress is on track.

When you delegate effectively, it allows you to focus on higher-priority tasks, and it gives your team members opportunities to grow and shine.

Step 3: Setting Boundaries to Prevent Burnout

Setting boundaries at work is crucial, especially in today's culture of constant connectivity. I found that one of the biggest challenges in managing my workload was the blurring of lines between work hours and personal time. As I started working longer hours, I noticed the toll it took on my health and relationships. That's when I realized if I didn't set clear boundaries, no one would do it for me.

Why Boundaries Matter

Boundaries help us manage stress, protect our well-being, and stay productive. Without them, we risk Burnout and a decline in our work quality. Here's what setting boundaries looked like for me:

- **Define working hours and stick to them:** I began setting a hard stop for myself. If my work hours were 9-6, I aimed to wrap up and log off by 6, even if I hadn't completed everything on my list. Surprisingly, this didn't hurt my productivity – it actually made me more efficient because I worked with a sense of urgency.

- **Learn to say no:** This was a tough one, but I started practicing the art of saying *'no'* or *'not right now'* to tasks that weren't a priority. I also learned to negotiate deadlines when my plate was already full.

- **Protect your time for deep work:** I started blocking off 'focus time' on my calendar. During these blocks, I turned off email notifications, silenced my phone, and concentrated on complex tasks without distractions.

How to Communicate Boundaries

Setting boundaries also means communicating them with your team and supervisors. For example, if you decide not to check emails after hours, make this clear to your colleagues so they know when they can expect a response.

A simple statement like, *'I try to prioritize personal time after 6 PM, so I will respond to emails first thing in the morning,'* can go a long way in managing expectations.

Putting It All Together

Managing an overwhelming workload is not about doing more but about doing the right things with intention. Prioritizing, delegating, and setting boundaries work together to help you stay productive without compromising your well-being. It took me time and a lot of trial and error, but these tools have become the foundation of my approach to work.

By prioritizing, I was able to focus on tasks that truly mattered. Delegation empowered my team and freed up my time for strategic thinking. Setting boundaries allowed me to recharge, stay creative, and protect my mental health. As I have continued to use these strategies, I have found that they don't just reduce stress, they actually increase my productivity and satisfaction at work.

Your Turn: Taking the First Step

If you are feeling overwhelmed, take a moment to breathe. Remember that no one expects you to do everything perfectly, and managing your workload is a skill that improves over time. Start small: try categorizing your tasks, find a task to delegate, or define one new boundary for yourself. Experiment with these tools and see what resonates best for you.

And here's a final reminder – it's not about working harder. It's about working smarter.

When you prioritize, delegate, and set boundaries, you create space to do your best work and, most importantly, to enjoy the journey.

'Balance isn't something you find, it's something you create.'

30.

Navigating Cross-Functional Teams

In teams where voices intertwine,
Different paths can brightly shine.
With open minds and hearts to share,
We weave solutions with thoughtful care.
Through varied views, our strength we find,
Together, we rise, our goals aligned.

'Collaboration is not about reaching the same viewpoint, but about building something meaningful from different perspectives.'

As working across departments has become the norm, Cross-functional teams bring together people with diverse expertise, perspectives, and priorities. They can be incredibly effective at solving complex problems, but they can also present unique challenges.

I am sure many of you, like I have, have felt the tension when working with people from other departments who don't necessarily share your goals or communication style. It can sometimes feel like you are speaking different languages or pulling in various directions. However, with the right approach, these differences can be a decisive advantage rather than a source of frustration. Let's look at some strategies for making the most of cross-functional teamwork, drawing from my own experience along the way.

Why Cross-Functional Teams Can Be Challenging

In a cross-functional team, every department brings its own goals and priorities. Marketing may focus on customer acquisition, while product development is concerned with usability, and finance is focused on staying within budget. When I first started working on cross-functional projects, I quickly discovered that people weren't always on the same page. The goals of my team in product development often didn't align with those of the marketing team, and our differing timelines and expectations made it difficult to find common ground.

In one instance, our event team wanted to launch a new space quickly to meet a promotional deadline. But, the product team knew that rushing it could lead to quality issues. This difference in priorities put us in a difficult situation. I learned that if I wanted to make this project successful, I needed to understand each team's perspectives and build bridges rather than walls.

Step 1: Embrace the Value of Diverse Perspectives

One of the most valuable lessons I have learned is that different perspectives lead to better decisions.

Each department brings unique expertise that's essential for the project's success. In the example above, the event team wanted a fast launch to meet their deadlines. At the same time, the product team was focused on quality. Initially, it felt like an impossible divide, but I soon realized that both perspectives were critical. The event team understood the importance of timeliness, and they, in product development, understood the need for quality. When we combined both insights, we were able to compromise on a timeline that balanced both needs.

Acknowledging Different Priorities

Everyone has different priorities, and that's okay. The key is acknowledging these priorities and finding where they overlap. I started by asking questions like, *'What's your biggest concern with this project?'* and *'What does success look like for your team?'* By listening to everyone's goals, I was able to see where our priorities aligned and where they didn't. Once we had that clarity, it became much easier to find solutions that satisfied both teams.

Step 2: Building Effective Communication Channels

Good communication is the cornerstone of cross-functional teamwork. Without it, misunderstandings, delays, and frustration are bound to occur. In my early experiences with cross-functional teams, I made the mistake of assuming that everyone understood my updates and concerns. However, as it turns out, each department has its own way of communicating, and what makes sense to one team may not be apparent to another.

Adapting Communication Styles

I realized that I needed to adapt my communication style to suit each team. For example, the finance team preferred detailed, numbers-driven reports. In contrast, the design team valued big-picture ideas and didn't want to be bogged down by details of numbers. By tailoring my communication to meet each team's preferences, I was able to get my points across more effectively and prevent misunderstandings.

Here are a few strategies that worked for me:

- **Set clear expectations at the start:** Before diving into the project, take the time to discuss communication preferences. For example, decide how frequently you will meet, whether updates will be via email or Slack, and what format everyone prefers.
- **Use visual aids:** Charts, graphs, and mockups can go a long way in bridging gaps, especially when working with departments like finance and creative, who may interpret information differently.
- **Be transparent and keep everyone in the loop:** Avoid assumptions. Provide regular updates to the entire team and make sure everyone is aware of any changes or challenges. This helps prevent surprises down the road.

Establishing a Common Language

I also found that establishing a *'common language'* was crucial. Different departments often use jargon that can be not very clear to others. For example, the product team might talk about *'sprints'* and *'user stories,'* while marketing discusses *'conversion rates'* and *'leads.'* In my project meetings, I started holding brief *'terminology'* sessions to explain key terms. This practice made a huge difference, helping everyone feel more included and reducing confusion.

Step 3: Building Trust Across Departments

Trust is the foundation of any successful team, but it's essential in cross-functional groups. When people trust each other, they are more likely to share ideas, take risks, and support each other's goals. In my cross-functional project, trust was something that developed gradually, but it made all the difference.

Start by Building Relationships

I took the time to build individual relationships with team members from each department. This didn't mean long lunches or bonding exercises. Instead, I made a conscious effort to learn about their roles, understand their challenges, and offer my support when needed. For example, when the marketing team was struggling with a resource constraint, I offered to help by reassigning some of our product development resources temporarily. This small gesture showed them that I was committed to the success of the entire project, not just my own team's goals.

Encourage Open Feedback

Creating a culture where people feel comfortable giving feedback is also essential. I started by regularly asking for feedback from the team, showing that I valued their input and was willing to make adjustments. As a result, other team members began to feel more comfortable voicing their concerns, which helped us identify and resolve issues early on.

Step 4: Finding Solutions Through Compromise

Cross-functional teams require a willingness to compromise. As I learned firsthand, compromise doesn't mean giving up on your goals, it means finding a solution that works for everyone involved. In our project, the product team wanted more time to ensure quality, while marketing was pushing for an earlier launch date. After discussing our priorities, we came to a compromise: we would launch a limited version of the product for the promotional event, with a plan to release additional features in a second phase. This solution allowed marketing to meet their deadline while giving the product team the time needed for a quality release.

Practicing Flexibility

It's essential to stay flexible. Sometimes, unexpected obstacles require us to adjust our plans, and when that happens, rigidity only leads to frustration. I encouraged my team to keep an open mind and look for solutions rather than focusing on problems. By adopting this mindset, we were able to adapt quickly and keep the project moving forward.

Step 5: Celebrating Wins Together

One of the best ways to reinforce teamwork is by celebrating successes as a group. Cross-functional teams often work hard, but they rarely get the chance to acknowledge their achievements together. When our project finally launched, I made sure to organize a small celebration where everyone could see how their efforts contributed to the final result. By celebrating as a group, we recognized the value each department brought to the project and strengthened our relationships for future collaborations.

Putting It All Together

Navigating cross-functional teams can be challenging, but it's also an incredible opportunity for growth. By embracing diverse perspectives, establishing effective communication, building trust, and practicing compromise, we can turn potential conflicts into powerful collaborations. In my own experience, these principles transformed my approach to cross-functional teamwork, helping me work more effectively and achieve better results.

If you are currently part of a cross-functional team, try incorporating some of these strategies. Take the time to understand each department's goals, adapt your communication style, and build trust with your teammates. Remember that you are all working towards the same end goal, and with the right approach, you can turn your differences into strengths.

Working with people from different departments isn't always easy. However, it can be one of the most rewarding aspects of your career, taking you from workplace hurdles to new heights.

'The best teams are built on diversity of thought, where every voice contributes to the harmony of success.'

Conclusion: Embracing the Climb

As we reach the end of this journey together, remember that every obstacle you encounter in the workplace is not merely a barrier but a stepping stone toward your personal and professional growth. Just as athletes train to overcome hurdles, you, too, can cultivate resilience and adaptability in the face of challenges.

The experiences, approaches and suggestions outlined in this guide are tools designed to empower you. They serve as a reminder that success is not a straight track but a winding road filled with bumps and turns. Embrace each hurdle as a chance to learn, adapt, and ultimately elevate yourself.

Reflect on your unique experiences and the hurdles you have faced. Each challenge has shaped you, honing your skills and fortifying your resolve. As you navigate your career, approach each obstacle with curiosity and courage. Ask yourself – *What can I learn from this? How can I turn this challenge into an advantage?*

In the words of Maya Angelou,

'You may encounter many defeats, but you must not be defeated.'

Let this be your mantra as you move forward. Believe in your capacity to rise above adversity and transform setbacks into triumphs.

Now, envision your future. Picture yourself standing at the summit of your career, having navigated the complexities of the workplace with grace and tenacity. Imagine looking back at the hurdles you have overcome, recognizing each one as a vital part of your journey. Each obstacle is transformed into a lesson learned, and every setback is a catalyst for growth.

As you embark on your journey as a Manager, remember that success is not solely defined by achievements but by the resilience you display and the growth you achieve along the way. With each hurdle you overcome, you are not just reaching for new heights – you are paving the way for others to follow.

Armed with the knowledge and strategies from this book, you are ready to tackle whatever challenges come your way. And, whenever you find yourself facing a specific hurdle, remember that you can always return to the relevant chapter for guidance and support.

So, embrace the climb, celebrate your victories, and continue to transform your challenges into stepping stones for success. The heights you can reach are limited only by your vision, determination, and willingness to keep moving forward.

Now, go forth and turn every obstacle into an opportunity. Your journey to success has only just begun.

About the Author

Nagesh Ramamurthy is a seasoned project management expert with over 35 years of leadership experience across a spectrum of organizations – from agile startups to global corporations.

Throughout his career, he has held influential positions that have shaped his understanding of the complex challenges leaders face in organizational environment.

His hands-on experience in guiding diverse teams through change has given him a unique perspective on the dynamics that drive organizational success.

Nagesh's career is marked by his practical approach to transforming obstacles into growth opportunities. As a trusted **leader and mentor**, he has consistently empowered teams to adapt, innovate, and achieve results, even in the most challenging environments.

Nagesh Ramamurthy is an **educator and experienced speaker** known for empowering Managers with actionable insights on adaptive growth.

Through a blend of strategic **consulting**, targeted **workshops**, and tailored **coaching**, Nagesh equips professionals with tools to build resilience, foster collaboration, and turn change into a powerful asset.

Readers will find his insights both credible and highly applicable, as he brings the wisdom of a seasoned leader, making him an essential guide for anyone aiming to excel in today's dynamic workplace.

www.ingramcontent.com/pod-product-compliance
Lightning Source LLC
LaVergne TN
LVHW091255150826
845673LV00006B/1431

* 9 7 9 8 8 9 6 1 0 4 3 7 7 *